What students say about **Sta**

*"Everything about going to university is made so
thought of doing and the double*

*"I really enjoyed reading this book. I LOVE that both sides (positive and negative) of
social media are highlighted. And listing the different places you can reach out to if
you're really struggling is great – it highlights that there are lots of options!"*

"This book is so reassuring and provides amazing advice for all aspects of university life."

*"I finished the book in one night – I couldn't put it down. So much information I didn't
know about. Thank you for the suggestions, they were needed."*

"I will forever recommend this book! It helped me so much when starting uni."

What parents say about **Starting University**

*"So many things to think about in such an easy-to-read format. I love the checklist and
ticking it off twice – great idea to help feel in control of jumping off the precipice into the
unknown. I wish I'd had this book when I went off to university – it would have made my
first year so much easier!"*

*"I want my daughter to embrace everything at university. This student guide is a great
resource which can be read in one sitting or dipped into when needed."*

*"A must for all students starting university. This book brilliantly covers off every angle in
practical and positive detail."*

*"This is amazing. Totally understandable even to a non-uni-goer like me. So well written
and I think both students and their parents would benefit from reading it."*

*"This book is helpful on so many counts. I'm a planner and the timeline is really useful
in telling me what my daughter needs to do and by what date. Also, the money section
prepares us for how much we'll need to give her and how much she'll need to pay back
when she graduates. It's brilliant: one place to go for everything we need to know."*

First published in Great Britain in 2023 by Katelli Publishing
www.katelli.co.uk

British Library Cataloguing-in-Publication Data: a catalogue record for this book is available from the British Library
Paperback ISBN 978-1-9161027-5-0

The information in this book has been compiled by way of general guidance only. The author and the publisher shall have no liability or responsibility to any person or entity regarding any loss, damage, disruption or injury incurred, or alleged to have incurred, directly or indirectly by the information or suggestions contained in this book.

All brand names and product names used in this book are trade names, service marks and trade or registered trademarks of their respective owners. The author is not associated with any product or vendor mentioned in this book other than where explicitly stated.

THE ESSENTIAL STUDENT GUIDE

Starting University

What to Expect • How to Prepare • Go and Enjoy

by Melissa Scallan

Edited by Louise Salmon • Design and Illustrations by Molly Shields

To my family

Contents

8 Staying Safe At University 105

Introduction

You're getting ready for university – fantastic!

You're about to embark on one of the most exciting and life-changing phases of your life. Over the next few years you'll enjoy a range of new experiences, you'll make good friends, you'll become more independent and you'll also become more knowledgeable. And you won't be on your own: every year over half a million students enrol as first year undergraduates at universities in the UK.

This book is designed to help you by offering useful, reassuring and easy-to-read advice on what to expect, how to prepare, what to take with you and how to deal with many of the new experiences you'll face during your first year at a UK university.

Starting University is for everyone preparing for their first year at university. From friendships and relationships to study strategies and staying safe, it's all here. You'll find information on finances – where your money comes from, where it goes and, crucially, how to get more of it – plus advice on where to find support if you're finding things difficult. If you're moving to university, there's useful information on living away from home – from laundry and cooking to supermarket shopping and budgeting – as well as advice for students living at home. And there's a chapter for your parents, too.

Handy checklists can be found throughout the book. You won't need all of it and you might want to add to it, but it will give you a good basis from which to start. The list approach – 'got' and 'packed' – focuses the mind, removes some of the uncertainty around what to take, and gives you the pleasure of ticking things off (twice).

In compiling this guide, I reviewed the information provided by a wide range of organisations including UK universities; sixth form and further education colleges; student forums; higher education admissions, regulatory, news and analysis organisations; financial information providers; news organisations; physical and mental health service providers; drug, smoking and alcohol advisory services; government and affiliated organisations; and commercial providers of goods and services to students.

It was crucial that I heard directly from students themselves so I also carried out a programme of research amongst Freshers – first year undergraduates – attending universities in the UK. The research took the form of an online, semi-structured questionnaire, filled in on an anonymous basis, and undertaken during the Christmas break when students had experienced their first term at university. Over 300 students responded to the survey, sharing their highs and lows and the advice they would give to new students. Where appropriate, and with their permission, I've included their wise, witty and poignant comments throughout this guide. I've also retained a few comments from the earlier surveys, where I felt they're still relevant. These comments inform the content, bring the student experience to life, and the advice to new students – on how to thrive not just survive – is invaluable.

In writing this book, I also paid attention to observations and comments made by parents of new students, taking note of their concerns, experiences and recommendations.

Starting University is packed with information, advice and lists. I hope you find it helpful. Please contact me if you think I've missed something crucial, if you have a good suggestion or would like to comment on the book. I'd be very happy to hear from you.

Good luck at university. You're on an exciting journey!

Melissa

Instagram: TheEssentialStudentGuide
Facebook: TheEssentialStudentGuide

Notes:

- For the sake of readability, I've used the term 'university' to refer to all higher education providers, 'A levels' to refer to all pre-higher education exams, 'undergraduates' to refer to those attending higher education institutions studying for their first degree or similar, and 'parents' to include parents, carers and guardians.

- Dates, links to websites and telephone numbers were correct at the time of printing. See End Notes for links to websites and licences

- Where I've mentioned brands or organisations, it's because I think the product or service is particularly useful or helpful. I'd be happy to hear from you if you have a recommendation for a product or service – and what makes it so good

Countdown To Leaving

This seasonal timeline indicates what generally happens and when during the academic year prior to going to university to study as a full-time undergraduate student in the UK. There may be individual differences that reflect your personal circumstances, the course or the university.

Additional elements such as admission tests, interviews, auditions, preparation of a portfolio or early deadlines, may be applicable depending on the course you're applying for or the university you're applying to.

It's important to check specific dates, deadlines and individual requirements with each university and course you're considering, with your school or college, and with UCAS: the Universities and Colleges Admissions Service.

Autumn (normally Year 13) . . . .

- Attend university Open Days for any universities you're considering that you didn't see during Year 12
- Edit and finalise your university application/personal statement
  - This explains to the university why you'd like to study a particular course or subject and what skills or experiences you have in that area
  - And it's the place to tell the universities anything about you that will help them put your achievements and experiences into context
  - Don't be tempted to plagiarise: UCAS uses sophisticated computer software to detect copied text
- Give your school/college enough time to read your application, check your qualifications, write and attach their comments/reference
- Have you considered other degree options? E.g. a sponsored degree, a degree apprenticeship or an accelerated degree
- Choose up to five courses to apply for
  - This is the limit under the UK system
  - Be realistic in your course choices. Your school or college will

tell you your predicted grades. Compare these to the published grades that universities normally require from students to study specific courses. You should apply for courses you have a good chance of getting a place on

- Choose courses with higher and lower grade requirements so that you'll have an insurance/back-up option
- UCAS normally starts to accept applications in September for most undergraduate courses
  - Don't delay as universities start sending out offers within weeks of receiving applications
  - Universities have until the May deadline to inform you of their decision (on January applications) so it can be a long wait
- Any course at the universities of Oxford and Cambridge and for most courses in medicine, veterinary medicine/science, dentistry, and music courses at conservatoires require early application to UCAS (the deadline is normally October)
- For conservatoires, check their websites or contact them for application dates
- Some universities and some courses may invite you to interview, audition or sit their own admission test

Winter ······························

- Start to receive decisions
- January is normally the UCAS deadline for the majority of university applications (note the deadline for early application above). It's possible to apply after this date but course choices may be limited and decision times will change
- If you're an international student, most universities will continue to accept applications (other than for early application courses) until later in the year
- If you included five choices on your application but have not received any offers – or you declined the offers you received – you can normally apply to UCAS Extra in February for an additional course

Spring

- Continue to receive decisions from universities
- Universities that have made you an offer may invite you to attend an Offer Holder Open Day. The day normally includes an introduction to the department, information about your course, a tour of the department/campus, taster lectures, and meeting staff and current students
- Accept or decline your offers; normally keeping a firm (first choice) and insurance (back-up) offer
- If you firmly accept an unconditional offer
    - You're normally committed to going to that university so you can't make an insurance choice, or be entered into Clearing
    - If you're sitting exams, it's really important that you keep working and get the best results you can
- Apply for university accommodation, if required
- Apply for student loans, and government grants and allowances, if required and if you're eligible. Investigate other grants, awards, scholarships and bursaries

Summer

- If you're sitting exams – good luck!
- Start practising – or improving – useful life skills, particularly if you're moving away from home for university e.g. cooking, laundry, supermarket shopping
- Work, work, work – save, save, save! Build up your savings by undertaking paid work
- Results Day. This is particularly important if your place at university is conditional on you achieving certain A level grades
    - Depending on what you're studying, schools and colleges will receive results on different dates – check when your results will be available
    - UCAS Hub updates at 8am on Results Day showing whether

you've been accepted onto your firm or insurance course (if no decisions are showing, contact your universities)
- If a place on a course is offered: accept or decline
- If you didn't meet the conditions of your offer, the university may still offer you a place, or a place on an alternative course
- If you've not received any university offers – or none you wanted – then you can apply for a course that still has spaces through UCAS Clearing
- If you receive your results prior to A level Results Day, and you don't have an offer of a place at university, you can enter Clearing early since it opens in July. However, most Clearing vacancies won't be published until August so you'll need to wait until then if you want to see the full selection of places that are available
- Fingers crossed: you're getting ready to go to university!

"Everyone is in the same situation you are, so try not to stress about starting uni :)"

1

How Are You Feeling?

The days are flying by and your first day at university is getting closer. How are you feeling?

Can't Wait!

Hopefully you're pretty excited about starting university.

- If you've attended the same school or lived in the same place for a long time, you could be completely ready to experience a new environment

- If you're moving away to go to university, maybe you're keen to leave home: to strike out on your own, to experience freedom, be independent

- Perhaps you loved what you saw during the university Open Days or what other people have told you about university life

- Maybe you're excited about your course or you're keen to take the next steps towards your future career

- If you're not too happy at home, school, college or work then going to university could be a great move

- Or perhaps you're just looking forward to a new beginning

And if you've taken a gap year, travelled, worked or you're used to looking after yourself – managing your money, getting yourself to places, doing your own shopping, cooking, laundry and cleaning – then, great! That's one part of the student experience that many Freshers find challenging – and you've already got it nailed.

Bit Worried About Leaving Home

Perhaps you're in the sixth form or attending a further education college, living at home but on the verge of moving out. If your parents help with many aspects of day-to-day living, and you're leaving home to go to university, you might have some concerns about being away from them.

It's possible your parents help you with:

- Food: making healthy choices, buying it, cooking it, clearing it away. No thought of food may have passed through your mind other than scouring cupboards when you're starving and preferring some foods over others

- Clothes: buying most of your 'essentials' such as jackets, jeans, trainers and underwear. They might also collect those clothes from the floordrobe, wash them, hang them out, iron them and return them to your room

- Transport: if you live somewhere that doesn't have very good public transport, they may be driving you places. Even if you can drive and have access to a car, you might still avail yourself of this great service

- Cleaning: providing you with clean bed sheets and towels and replacing bathroom essentials when they run out. And, even if you're responsible for your bedroom (or your part of it), they probably keep the rest of the home clean and tidy

- Bank of Mum and Dad: it's likely that, in addition to providing your bed and board, they might give you an allowance, pay or contribute towards a phone, a computer, travel costs, clothes, school-related costs, health, eye and dental costs. They might pay when things need fixing and lend you money when you don't have your card or cash on you (do you sometimes forget to pay it back?)

- And hopefully they're supportive: listening to you when you feel like talking, making reasonable suggestions that you may or may not take, and picking you up when you're feeling down

If this sounds like you, then you might have concerns around:

- Sticking to a budget: you might never have had to restrict your spending or divide up your money into things like rent, food, travel and laundry

- Making household decisions on stuff like food, cleaning and tackling clothes washing

- Making decisions without using your parents as a sounding board

- Being apart from them for any length of time

- You might even be worried about how your parents will cope without you

Other Possible Concerns

You might also have some other concerns, such as:

- If you're moving away then you might be wondering whether you'll like your accommodation and who your flatmates will be

- You're undoubtedly hoping you'll quickly find friends

- What about a girlfriend or boyfriend? If you're travelling some distance, you might be leaving someone important behind. Or perhaps you're hoping to find someone

- Given the cost and importance of going to university, you might be wondering whether you've chosen the right course, the right university, the right location and if you'll enjoy it

- And what if you're an international student? You might be concerned about being geographically distant from your support network, possibly having to study and socialise in a foreign language, and maybe understanding and adopting different cultural norms. You might be feeling the weight of your family's expectations and you're undoubtedly hoping that people will be friendly, welcoming and supportive

So, it's not unreasonable that you might be experiencing some anxiety. This book can't take away all those worries – which are quite natural and part of the process of helping you prepare for change – but, by providing you with practical advice and information, it can help to minimise some of your fears.

2

Important Things To Do Before The Start Of Term

This is a pretty comprehensive list of things to do. Don't worry if it doesn't all get done before you start – lots of things can be sorted out once you start university.

All New Students

- Set up your student bank account

    - Student bank accounts aren't compulsory but they do tend to offer helpful features e.g. fee-free and interest-free overdraft facilities. Some might offer you a freebie to join them e.g. a travel card
    - You may have to wait until your university place is confirmed to complete the application process
    - Once you have your bank account, set up online banking so you can check your balance and you can contact the bank if (when) you mislay your bank card

    "I lost my debit card. It could be in one of two nightclubs or three taxis...."

- International students: you may only be able to set up a UK bank account once you arrive in the UK. In which case, bring cash, credit, debit or prepaid cards to tide you over until the application process is complete

- Student loans

  - If you're eligible, and if you require them, you can apply for UK government student loans: the tuition fee loan and the maintenance loan
  - You can start this process early (normally from March of the year you're intending to go to university) and you don't need a confirmed place to apply
  - It can take up to six weeks for loans to come through so, if you want the money in your bank account when you start the course, it's best not to delay applying. However, you can apply for loans up to nine months after the first day of the academic year for your course
  - You may be eligible for additional government-provided financial support. You can apply for this when you apply for student loans
  - If you're eligible, you can get a maintenance loan whether you're living in a hall of residence, in private accommodation or if you're living at home
  - Go to https://www.gov.uk/apply-for-student-finance and follow the links, as appropriate

- Finances in general: think about any alternative/additional funding

  - It's possible that any maintenance loan may not be sufficient even to cover accommodation costs so you should consider other ways you could fund your time at university (read Chapter 7: Money)
  - If your parents are contributing, then agree how much and how often they will transfer money. It may help with budgeting to receive money from them on a weekly basis (read Chapter 10: Parents – for a suggestion on parental contribution)

- Talk to your parents or teachers about managing your finances e.g. budgeting, bills, ways of saving money, overdrafts
- Try to find or increase your paid work in order to build up your savings. Being a student – whether it's socialising with your new friends or managing living costs – is nearly always more expensive than you anticipate. According to student news site The Tab, Freshers' Week alone – with club entry, pre-drinks, taxis, drinking, fancy dress, hangover food, society sign-ups and the weekly shop – can come to over £400

"Save money before going so that you don't have as many money issues whilst at university. Even if it's just £100–£200 it'll help massively."

"Have savings behind you so you can participate in events you may not have budgeted for."

- When you receive written confirmation of your place from the university, read through the letter

  - There may be specific things you need to do e.g. you may need to send the university proof of your qualifications or provide evidence of passing a health check or DBS clearance, if that's required for your course
  - Accept your place at the university. You'll then begin receiving information from the university such as your student ID card, registration details, course or module choices, accommodation details, your university email address, Freshers' or Welcome Week information

- Get ready for the start of term

  - Read through any information sent by your department – there may be materials they'd like you to prepare in advance, books to read or equipment you need to buy

- Look online and see where things are e.g. your term-time address, your academic department, the leisure centre/sports facilities, the Student Union, your nearest supermarket, medical centre, support services
- Figure out how you're going to get to around e.g. bike, bus, walk, train

- Start finding your friends

  - You can start finding your university friends even before term starts. Most universities have moderated social media accounts for new students – often Facebook. The university may send you a link (if there's an official page) or you can look online and search University of X Freshers (or Offer Holders or Applicants) and year of entry. You could look when your place is confirmed – or sooner if you're feeling confident or just curious
  - You'll find your future hall/block/college/flatmates, people studying the same course as you, and discover clubs and societies you might be interested in joining
  - You'll normally be funnelled into a WhatsApp or Snapchat group chat so update your socials
  - If you feel awkward or shy, you can start off by just reading the comments – you don't have to contribute unless/until you want to. But do try and join in: everyone's new and keen to make friends and you'll soon find yourself in group chats
  - Getting to know names, faces and a bit about people ahead of time is reassuring – and exciting too

"Try to talk to people online beforehand. It makes you feel a lot more comfortable when you move and you may even make some friends."

"Try to make friends before you move, get to know people in your accommodation. All you need is a good group of people to vibe with and you'll be alright."

- General health

  - Make sure your vaccinations are up-to-date e.g. MMR, meningitis ACWY. You'll be coming into contact with a lot of new people, some of whom may unknowingly be carriers of illnesses
  - Diarise booking a flu jab in the autumn, especially if you're an 'at risk' person e.g. asthmatic

- If you have any mental or physical health needs

  - Tell your home therapist/GP about your plans so they can help prepare you for the transition
  - They can also let the university know in advance about your needs to ensure speedy access to services/continuity of care
  - You may be eligible for additional financial support e.g. Disabled Students' Allowance. You can apply for this when you apply for student loans. Allow yourself time to make the application since you might need to provide evidence

- See the Important Documents Checklist at the end of this chapter for vital information to gather before the start of term

- Sort out your essentials and stationery – see the lists at the end of this chapter for suggestions

- Read this book; have a roam around your university's website e.g. your department, clubs and societies, the Students' Union, the library, support services; look at the university's social media; talk to other people who've gone to university

If You're Living Away From Home

- Your accommodation options and the process for applying to live away from home are outlined in Chapter 3: Your Living Arrangements

- If university accommodation is offered, accept (or reject) the offer. If you reject it, follow the university's advice on what you need to do to find alternative accommodation

- Undertake all the necessary admin

  - Write down your term-time address and look up how to get there
  - Confirm your moving-in day and time
  - See what's provided in your hall/flat/room so you know what to take
  - Pay your deposit (usually up to one month's rent)
  - Set up a standing order to pay your rent (and possibly household bills, if not included in your rent)
  - Read Chapter 3: Your Living Arrangements

- General health

  - Students normally register with their university GP so you need to gather various pieces of information to give to the university surgery/health centre e.g. your NHS number, your home GP's details, any medication you regularly take, your immunisation history (which you can normally get from your home GP)
  - Visit your home GP and get a month's worth of any repeat/regular medication so you're fully stocked up until you register with the university GP
  - Visit your home dentist and optician and get any work done before you leave

If you're unwell when you're away from your university GP e.g. during a visit home, you can request an appointment with the nearest GP practice. You can receive emergency treatment for 14 days but after that you'll have to register as a temporary resident or permanent patient

- If you have any mental or physical health needs, let the university know in advance. They may allow you to move into your term-time accommodation a few days early so you can settle and make contact with student support services

- Gather together everything you need to take with you (see the lists within each chapter)

> *If, on arrival at university, you discover you don't have something, seriously don't worry: chances are you can get it from a local shop, order it online, borrow it or improvise*

- If you've bought anything new to take with you

  - Open items up and check them, especially anything electrical
  - Remove any packaging – this will reduce the space required for transporting them
  - Wash any new bedding or towels so they smell nice

- Investigate whether you need any specific contents insurance

  - A university hall of residence might provide contents insurance but this might be restricted to items lost or damaged within a locked room or within the hall
  - Additional insurance might be necessary for expensive possessions such as a bike, musical instrument, phone or laptop

- Decide whether or not you need a television licence

  - If you're living in university accommodation, you'll need a television licence to watch TV in your own room. Shared areas may already be covered by a television licence

- However, if you live at another address outside term time (e.g. with your parents), you're covered by a valid licence at their address if the device you're using to watch television is battery powered, not plugged into the mains and not connected to an aerial
- For more information: https://www.gov.uk/tv-licence

- Food and drink

  - If you don't prepare meals very often, practise cooking some quick and tasty meals from scratch

"Start thinking about day-to-day life before you go then it won't come as a shock…. Every now and then just think 'If I had to eat something now and my parents weren't around, what would I do?'"

"Have five dishes you can comfortably cook, and know the time they take to cook and the price."

- Read Chapter 5: Food & Drink – suggestions of what to eat and some easy recipes
- If you don't already shop for food, do some supermarket shopping as this will be useful practice for when you're on your own. For example, you'll see how supermarkets are laid out, how to find items and what they cost
- If your nearest term-time supermarket is far away, you could practise ordering groceries online so you're familiar with the service provided e.g. how to navigate the website, see the actual cost of items and the delivery cost, and see how frequently it delivers to your area (you can add your term-time address and see the impact on frequency)
- Read how to Shop Savvy in Chapter 7

- If you don't already do it, learn how to do laundry

  - At the very least, you need to know how to use the washing machine
  - Read Chapter 4: Laundry

- See what taxi services operate in your university area

  - Your university may have a list of recommended taxi firms
  - If it's an online service, and you're not already a customer, you could try using it so you're familiar with how the service works
  - Taking a taxi might sound extravagant but sharing a ride with friends can be as little as £1/person

- If you're an international student, in addition to the above, there may be other things that you need to arrange in advance, such as:

  - Visa
  - Passport
  - Health insurance
  - Travel insurance
  - Proof of finance
  - Proof of address: in the UK and your home address
  - Confirmation of acceptance of studies
  - A SIM card to make local calls from your phone (if your phone is unlocked)
  - Set up web-based accounts so you can make calls for free over the internet (except for any web access costs) when you and the other person are both online and using the same service e.g. WhatsApp, FaceTime, Skype
  - Investigate what your university organises specifically for its international students, such as welcome and orientation events, International Halls, dedicated social media, student welfare, language lessons or a general support service

DOCUMENT CHECKLIST

	Got	Packed
Offer letter from the university		
Term-time accommodation address and how to get there		
Accommodation tenancy agreement		
Campus map		
Exam certificates		
Student loan/funding details		
Bank account details: regular and student accounts		
Any bursary/scholarship/sponsorship/grant/award documentation		
ID in the form of driving licence/provisional licence/passport		
National Insurance details		
Any insurance documents/details		
TV licence, if necessary		

Health information including:

	Got	Packed
Home GP details: name, address, telephone number		
NHS number		
Medication taken regularly: name, dosage, frequency, when to be renewed, etc		
Copy of immunisation record		
Any current health information e.g. copy of glasses prescription		

International students might also need:

	Got	Packed
Visa		
Passport		
Birth certificate		
Travel documents		
Health insurance		
Travel insurance		
Funding documents		

ESSENTIALS CHECKLIST

	Got	Packed
Phone plus charging cable		
Laptop/computer plus charging cable		
Multi-USB plug adapter e.g. IKEA KOPPLA		
Multi-socket extension lead		
Headphones/earphones (plus charging cable, if required) – noise cancelling ones might be useful		
Portable speaker plus charging cable		
Portable charger plus charging cable		
Printer plus charging cable, ink cartridges and printer paper		
USB memory stick		
Ear plugs		
Cash		
Debit card		
Rail/coach card		
Student ID card		
Store/loyalty cards		
Planner/diary (academic diaries start in September)		
International students will need plug adapters, SIM card		

STATIONERY CHECKLIST

	Got	Packed
Files/folders		
Pads of paper of various types e.g. A4, ruled, graph, plain		
Textbooks		
Pens		
Pencils		
Sticky tape in a dispenser		
Scissors		
Highlighters		
Ruler		
Hole punch		
Pencil sharpener		
Eraser		
Stapler		
Glue		
Paper clips		
Sticky notes		
Sticky tack		
Calculator		
Plastic wallets		
Course-specific items		
Pencil case		

3

Your Living Arrangements

Living Away From Home

Typically, the majority of undergraduate students, who study in the UK, live away from home during term time.

Freedom!

When I asked the first-year students in my research what they liked most about being at university, living away from home was one of the most common answers they gave. They enjoy the freedom that comes from no longer living under their parents' roof – and not having to abide by their parents' rules. Enjoy!

"Being able to do whatever you want, whenever you want, and not having to say when you're going somewhere or check plans with your parents."

"The 'freedom' of being away from your parents. You're able to get up when you want, eat what you want, when you want, manage money, etc. Really start to feel like an adult and learn how to live alone!"

"Feeling independent and being able to do things in your own time - work, social, fitness etc."

"The freedom you get! It's a time when you can really focus on yourself and do what you want to do :)"

Typical First Year Accommodation

If you're living away from home, your choice of accommodation will generally fall into one of the following three options: university hall of residence, private hall of residence and privately rented accommodation.

University Halls of Residence

It's good to view a few halls of residence during university Open Days (or via the website), to get an idea of how they're set up.

- Halls of residences are often quite similar: usually flats of varying sizes with multiple single-occupation study bedrooms with either en suites or shared bathrooms and there's often a communal kitchen/dining area. Study bedrooms in older halls might be situated off long corridors

- WiFi is normally included and there's usually a launderette on site. In larger halls, facilities might include a shop, a bar, a gym and a canteen. But services and facilities provided in halls vary widely between, and within, universities

- There's usually an on-site warden – either a member of staff or an older student – who can offer advice, support and possibly first aid

- Rooms in halls tend to be the most popular option. They're usually close to the university, the rent tends to include utilities (and sometimes food), which makes it easier to budget, and you'd be living with other students from your university

- If you choose the catered option, there might be a dining room where meals are served or there may be various places around the university where you can eat, using a prepaid card. Meals may not be provided three times a day, seven days a week, and there'll be times when you don't want to, or aren't able to, go out to eat. You should, therefore, bring some cutlery, crockery and basic cooking equipment

- To secure your room, you'll usually be asked to pay a deposit. You'll then normally pay your rent at the beginning of each term

Private Halls of Residence

Private halls of residence are owned and managed by a private provider that specialises in student accommodation.

- The accommodation is often similar in style to university halls of residences i.e. flats or rooms with shared facilities

- Sometimes the facilities may be newer or more luxurious than those found in the university-owned halls. If the facilities are better, it's likely the rent will also be higher

- Check what's included in your rent e.g. utilities

- You may be living with students attending other local universities

Privately Rented Accommodation

You may have applied for university accommodation but not been allocated a room or you may simply prefer to live in privately rented accommodation.

- Contact the university accommodation service for advice since it normally helps students with privately rented accommodation. The department may:

- Provide a list of letting agents, private landlords or flat share lists
- Identify which are the popular student areas
- Give advice on current rent levels and paying deposits
- Offer information on housing regulation and other aspects of a private sector tenancy e.g. gas safety certificate, the rent deposit scheme, registering for council tax exemption
- Offer a contract-checking service

- If possible, try to visit the property in person. Amongst other things, you can check its condition, see how long it takes you to get to the university during rush hour and speak to existing tenants

- You normally pay your rent on a monthly basis (in advance). Utilities, e.g. gas and electricity, are usually paid separately

Applying For University And Private Halls Of Residences

Check when you can apply for accommodation; often you can apply once you've made the university your firm (first) choice. Some universities allow applications where they're the insurance (back-up) option.

- Don't wait to apply. Universities tend to allocate places on a first come, first served basis and spaces in popular accommodation tend to fill up quickly

- You normally identify your top three or four preferred halls from a list – with your choices based on factors such as weekly cost, whether it has an en suite, whether it's catered or self-catered, distance from the university or faculty, whether you have any specific preferences/requirements

- It might be a good idea to apply for flats with a larger number of flatmates since you'll have a greater selection of people/potential friends to interact with, on a daily basis

- Many universities guarantee a place in halls to first year students

- Rooms in halls are normally allocated once your place at the university is confirmed

> You may be allocated a room in a hall that wasn't from your preferred list, that you've not had the opportunity to see in advance or, if you're going to university through Clearing, you may not have been given a choice in where you live. Don't worry too much as the accommodation options tend to be fairly similar to each other.
>
> "When you're actually on campus, what kind of room you have doesn't matter. It's the vibes and the people that matter the most."

- Hopefully you'll find yourself in a flat with nice people and you'll have positive experience of flatsharing

"Living in halls is one of the best experiences I've EVER had. And I hate leaving home, so that really is something."

"My flatmates are definitely the best part of my experience at university."

How Is Accommodation Allocated?

Although some universities allow you to go online and select a specific room in a hall from a list of what's available, it's more common for universities to allocate accommodation based on its own algorithms, whilst taking into account your preferences or needs.

- Some universities actively mix up students with regard to factors such as gender, age, religious beliefs, nationality, faculty, school type – even setting percentage targets for the different types of student. Similarly, some universities have a policy to separate students from the same school or college

- They reason that a valuable part of going to university is that students learn to mix with, and get to know, people whose lives and backgrounds are different to their own

- Some universities group Freshers with similar personality characteristics in order to ease the transition into university life. You might be asked about personality and lifestyle factors e.g. whether you're outgoing or reserved; an early-riser or night bird; a smoker or whether you drink alcohol; whether you're a vegetarian; tidy; sporty; like clubbing, etc
  - This approach suggests that if you're similar to your flatmates it's easier to connect with them, you'll experience less conflict, you'll settle more quickly and be less homesick

If the university asks you to fill in a questionnaire, be honest about your personality and lifestyle as this increases the likelihood of being grouped with people who you'll feel comfortable living with

- Some universities allow students to request accommodation: either by selecting a specific room or requesting a room in a hall, according to what the university can offer
  - This might include applying to share with existing friends; requesting a room in alcohol-free halls or halls that have quiet areas; single-sex flats or halls; an LGBTQ+ community; by vegan/vegetarian/halal requirements; by nationality; by age; within a 'green' community

- And if you have a particular need for a certain type of accommodation, universities normally make available some housing to serve students with specific requirements e.g. if you have a child, have a particular mental or physical requirement, are estranged and therefore need year-round accommodation, have a carer who lives with you

- Finally, some universities state all accommodation is randomly allocated

Unhappy With Your Accommodation?

If you don't like your accommodation, speak to the university accommodation service. They'll be able to advise you on your options and, where available, offer alternatives.

If you've already moved into a hall of residence, speak to the warden who may be able to resolve any issues. Whether in a hall or in a private residence there may be a fee to pay in order to break the contract and you may have to find someone to take your room. This, and any other information, should be in your tenancy agreement.

Your Study Bedroom

Whether moving into halls or privately rented accommodation, you're likely to be moving into a single room that will be your bedroom and study for the coming year.

It's likely to be simply furnished with a bed, mattress, mattress cover, bedside table, desk, chair, shelves, curtains, pin board and bin. Check the inventory as accommodation varies.

- Bedding
    - You usually provide your own bedding including pillows
    - You're likely to have limited storage so you could take just one set of bedding that you would wash and tumble dry on the same day
    - Include two sets of pillow cases – wash these more often
    - Check the size of your bed in advance so you know what size fitted sheet and how many pillows to bring. Even if you have a single bed, take a double duvet to wrap yourself up in
    - A mattress cover/protector is a good idea. It's hygienic and helps to ensure your mattress stays fresh and clean
    - A mattress topper (or a piece of foam the size of your mattress) provides extra cushioning and can make a bed more comfy

- Some universities sell bedding packs or suggest specialist private companies who can kit out your bedroom, kitchen and bathroom. UniKitOut (www.unikitout.com), working in partnership with over 280 universities and private housing providers, delivers ready-made student packs directly to your halls, before your arrival, and can deliver anywhere in the UK

- Clothes and accessories
    - Bring enough clothes – especially underwear – so you can last at least a week (if not two) without needing to do laundry
    - Bring dressing-up clothes as fancy dress parties are common.

"We've done a ton of theme nights: festival, black and white, Hawaiian...."

- If your hall hosts formal dinners, pack smart/evening wear
- Transport your clothes on their hangers in large bags so they'll be ready to hang when you arrive
- Your first term takes you into winter so pack warm clothes and a warm coat/jacket
- An oversized blanket/hoodie is a great idea to keep you warm and cosy when you're working in your room
- It's likely you'll be doing lots of walking to and from university so take a good bag/backpack to carry all your stuff
- Take shoes/trainers specifically for clubbing. And ones that you don't mind getting damaged

"A specific pair of shoes/trainers just for nightclub use that will get trashed."

- Pack flip flops/sliders for wearing in shared kitchens, bathrooms

"You need shoes to wear around the flat (floor is grim)."

- Create your own first aid kit; it's cheaper than buying a ready-made one and it will be filled with the things you know you'll actually use. And it's likely – with all the new people you'll meet and how busy you'll be – that you will get sick so make sure it includes painkillers, throat lozenges, etc

"Cold remedies (you will get ill immediately)."

- Bring a doorstop to prop your door open when you're in. It shows that you're welcoming and people can stop by and say hello

- Large under-bed storage boxes with lids are a good idea e.g. IKEA SOCKERBIT. You're likely to have limited storage so this is where you could put things you rarely use/extra bits

- You can create hanging shelves inside your wardrobe for extra storage e.g. IKEA STUK

- There's rarely enough space for your clothes so you could also bring a row of hooks to hang over a door

- Bring accessories from home to decorate your room e.g. cushions, photos, fairy lights, rug, potted plant, teddy bear, room spray. Something interesting or different could be a conversation-starter

"I got a rug for the floor and it makes the room 10x nicer (you know it's ' your dirt'...)."

"A teddy bear. Just makes times better."

"Decorations make your room feel like yours. Helps you feel more at home."

- A full-size clothes airer is useful for items that can't be tumbled and/or to save on drying costs. If you're moving into a hall of residence, there may be a drying room so you may not need a full size airer. A radiator airer for small items is also useful

- Hobbies/interests, to do in your room, that help you relax

  "Something to keep you entertained when you want to be by yourself, like books or games."

- Ear plugs and headphones are a good idea to screen out noises around you so you can concentrate, relax or sleep

  "Headphones because often the walls are thin."

- A lanyard/something to keep your keys safe

  "I lost my room key and they charged me £20 to replace it! That's a whole week of lunches."

- A whiteboard to help you stay organised and keep track of assignments, cleaning and shopping. And maybe a second, smaller, one to attach to your door for messages when you're out

- A large water bottle or jug for your room. Maybe one with a filter in case you don't like the taste of the local water

- A basket of snacks for your room

- A water bottle, that you can refill on campus and a travel mug, as coffee shops often offer discounts if you bring your own mug

- A sleeping bag and/or a mat is handy for when you have a friend staying over: single beds are common in student accommodation and there's not a lot of room for two

- A bag/suitcase on wheels for when you go home

- See the checklists at the end of this chapter for more suggestions

> *On arrival, check the room/inventory thoroughly, photograph any damaged/missing items and inform the accommodation management*

Kitchen

Whether you're self-catering or being catered for, you'll probably have access to a shared kitchen where you normally have to provide everything you might need (but check the inventory as some are well-equipped).

- Even if you choose the catered option, there'll be times when you don't want to go out to eat. You should, therefore, bring some basic crockery, cookware and ingredients for breakfasts, late night snacks and easy meals

- At minimum, bring mugs, glasses, tea, coffee, soft drinks, biscuits etc to share with your new flatmates and friends

- If you're cooking, then you'll need plates and bowls, cutlery, and implements to prepare and cook food e.g. sharp knife, vegetable peeler, chopping board, wooden spoons, large sieve and pans – as well as the food itself. See the Kitchen Checklist for suggestions

- It's a good idea to bring crockery, mugs and cutlery that are (a) distinctive so you can tell they're yours and (b) cheap as items often go missing

- Check what type of hob is in your kitchen as some pans won't work on some hobs

"Bring pans that work on all kinds of hobs because mine does not – so it's just a bowl with a handle now."

- A large pan is a good idea for cooking extra portions that you can store/ freeze/share

- And bring re-usable food containers to store leftovers/extra portions so you don't have to cook a whole new meal and for taking lunch on the days you're on campus: saving you time and money

"Pack lunches as food can be expensive and it's time-consuming to wait in line during lunch."

- If a parent is taking you to university, ask if they would take you to the supermarket nearest to where you're living so you can see where it is, how it's laid out and you can buy enough food to set you up for the first week (fingers crossed: they might even contribute towards that first supermarket shop). See the Useful Shopping List at the end of Chapter 5

- If you're in a chat with your new flatmates ahead of moving in together, you could discuss what's provided in the flat, what each of you has already and what you could buy together when you arrive. Otherwise you might end up having to store multiple kettles and toasters

- There might be a cleaning service as part of your hall package but they may only visit once a week and only clean communal areas. You'll therefore, on a regular basis, need to wash up whatever you've used and wipe down surfaces where things have spilled on a regular basis (dull but necessary). You'll need items for cleaning e.g. sponges, washing-up liquid, surface spray, kitchen towel

- Usually there's a broom, dustpan and brush, vacuum cleaner, mop and bucket, iron and ironing board provided (but do check)

- If you have a long-term condition such as diabetes, epilepsy or an allergy, tell your flatmates or your neighbours in your halls what your condition is and where vital medication is kept. You could keep medication and instructions in a labelled box in your kitchen cupboard – rather than in your locked room – so it's easily accessible in an emergency

Bathroom

You may have your own en suite or you may be sharing a bathroom

- You'll need to provide your own towels, bath mat and toiletries

- You may or may not be responsible for cleaning the bathroom, however it will be handy to have your own cleaning items e.g. sponges, cleaning spray, kitchen towel and bleach

- See the Bathroom Checklist for suggested items to bring

Being a Good Flatmate

You'll probably be living with your flatmates for the whole of the academic year. It's unlikely you'll have the same tolerance for dirt/mess/noise so you'll have to agree what's an acceptable level you can all try to work towards.

In the Kitchen

- Clear up after yourself: wash up, dry up (replace tea towels every day or whenever dirty), put items away, wipe up spills and crumbs

- If the surfaces are really dirty or greasy, first use kitchen roll to remove any spills then spray with a cleaner and wipe with a sponge

- When using the microwave, cover the food (e.g. with a piece of kitchen towel) to prevent splatters

- Don't take your flatmates' stuff without asking and replace what you borrow

- If the kitchen or recycling bins need emptying, take them out

- A cleaning rota is a good idea

In the Bathroom

- Leave it clean after using it – no-one likes a dirty, hairy bathroom

- Open a window/turn on the extractor fan whilst you're in the bathroom to let fresh air in and minimise the likelihood of mould growing

- Replace empty toilet rolls and make sure hand soap is available

- Replace the hand towel every few days

In Your Study Bedroom

- If you have your own room, you can be as untidy as you like but try not to be dirty: empty your bin, bring out used plates, cups etc otherwise you'll encourage bugs and your room will smell

- Study bedrooms are usually very close to each other so you should keep your noise down e.g. music on low, if you have friends to stay then keep the sound low, close doors quietly

General House Rules

- Keep the shared areas clean and clear of your stuff

- Keep on top of any shared costs e.g. have a kitty or take it in turns for joint purchases such as toilet roll, washing up liquid, sponges

- Agree house rules e.g. alcohol, smoking, drugs, noise, friends or partners staying over (whether or not, how often and for how long)

- Be nice to each other e.g. offer to make your flatmates a cup of tea or coffee, accept deliveries for them when they're out

Some Cleaning Tips

Washing Up by Hand

It's unlikely that you'll have a dishwasher in your student accommodation. Sadly, you're it.

- Scrape any food into a bin and run hot water over the items to remove any bits
    - Don't pour oil down the drain: pour it into a cup and let it harden before binning it or soak it up with kitchen roll and then put the paper in the bin

- Run HOT water into a (clean) bowl/sink and add a squirt of washing up liquid

- Using a sponge, wash the cleanest items first e.g. glasses and mugs
    - Ensure rims are sponged clean
    - Use non-stick sponges for non-stick pans otherwise you'll remove the non-stick coating

- Some items might need to be soaked before you can remove any burnt bits e.g. oven trays. If food is burnt into a pan or oven tray, add washing up liquid and hot water, then leave to soak for a few hours or overnight. The burnt bits should gradually lift away. Then wash as normal

- Rinse items under hot running water to check they're clean and the soap bubbles are removed

- Drying: use a clean tea towel to dry and then put away

- Wipe down the surfaces to finish

- Sweep the floor and wipe away any drips or spills for good measure

The Bathroom

- Vacuum the floor

- Basin and shower/bath: spray areas with bathroom cleaner and, using hot water and a sponge, wipe down

- Toilet and floor: spray areas with bathroom cleaner and use kitchen roll – which you can throw away afterwards – to wipe down

- Squirt bleach around the toilet bowl and leave it to soak

- Use different washing up gloves to those you use in the kitchen

Living At Home

You might opt to live at home, whilst studying at university. Perhaps you're attending a local university, and moving out seems unnecessary, or maybe it's simply something that you or your family prefer.

- You're likely to save money since it's usually cheaper to live at home than to rent from somebody else

- It might be easier and more convenient to live at home if your family takes care of things like food shopping, cooking or laundry

- Maybe you prefer the calm, the quiet or the familiarity of living at home. Some students find they get their work done more quickly at home as there are fewer distractions

- Maybe it keeps you closer to loved ones, a job or a home you're responsible for

It's possible you might miss out on some aspects of student life so there are strategies you can use to help you maximise your university experience whilst living at home:

- If possible, make arrangements every now and then, to stay with a friend who lives in student accommodation so you can join in a variety of social events

- Be proactive in making friends and join in, whenever you can. You might find you naturally drift towards other people who also live at home, since you have a shared experience

- Join study groups (in-person and/or online) so you can interact with your coursemates

- And join university-led sport and social clubs so you can find – and maintain – friendships with people who share your interests

- If you feel your parents aren't treating you as an adult then you need to find some resolution. Talk things through so you can find a way to live together peacefully and respectfully e.g. you could discuss and agree on house rules or show them the ways in which you're taking responsibility for yourself (See also Chapter 10: The Parents' Chapter)

- Let the university know if you need support with regard to living at home. For example, if there's a problem with internet access or you don't have enough data, or you're finding it difficult to concentrate or find a quiet space to work, or you feel unsafe or it's affecting your mental health. The university should offer advice, support and solutions

STUDY BEDROOM CHECKLIST

	Got	Packed
Pillows x 2		
Pillow cases x 4		
Duvet		
Duvet cover		
Fitted undersheet		
Mattress cover		
Mattress topper/foam		
Blanket		
Hot water bottle		
Bedside bin		
Bedside and desk lamps (plus bulbs)		
White board and pen		
Doorstop		
Under-bed storage e.g. IKEA SOCKERBIT		
Room decorations e.g. photos, fairy lights, cushions, potted plant, rug, teddy bear, room spray, diffuser		
Clothes hangers		
Wardrobe storage e.g. IKEA STUK		
Cleaning		
All-purpose cleaner		
Duster/cloths/kitchen roll		
Bin bags		

PERSONAL/HYGIENE CHECKLIST

	Got	Packed
Toothbrush & toothpaste		
Two-pin to three-pin plug adaptor for electric toothbrush		
Floss		
Brace/retainers and box		
Liquid hand soap		
Hand sanitizer		
Shower gel		
Shampoo & conditioner		
Cleanser		
Cotton wool		
Moisturisers – face and body		
Hair brush/comb		
Hair products & accessories		
Nail scissors and/or clippers		
Tissues: boxed and travel pack		
Ear buds		
Deodorant		
Other face/body creams		
Razors, shaving cream, hair removal items, tweezers		
Sanitary products		
Sunscreen		
Mirror		
Contraception		
Contact lenses, case & liquid		
Make-up		
Perfume/aftershave		
Prescription glasses and case		
Jewellery		
Hairdryer/straighteners		
Vitamins		

FIRST AID CHECKLIST

	Got	Packed
Plasters		
Antiseptic cream		
Ibuprofen		
Paracetamol		
Decongestant		
Throat lozenges		
Antihistamine – for allergies/bug bites/stings		
Specific personal medication		

OTHER USEFUL STUFF CHECKLIST

	Got	Packed
Hobby/interest e.g. books, computer games, consoles		
Playing cards, board games or other games		
Small sewing kit with needles and a variety of threads		
Lunch box		
Water bottle		
Travel mug		
Backpack		
Reusable shopping bags		
Bag/wheeled suitcase		
Slippers/sliders		
Lanyard for keys		
Musical instrument		
Bicycle and kit		
Sports kit and bag		
Umbrella		
Sleeping bag and/or mat		
Dressing up/fancy dress clothes		
Swimming costume, goggles and towel		
Dressing gown/bathrobe		
First term: winter clothes		
Formal/evening wear		

KITCHEN CHECKLIST

	Got	Packed
Plates – large and small x 2 of each		
Bowls x 2		
Cutlery		
Drinking glasses x 2		
Mugs – lots		
Pack of disposable cups for visitors		
Pans: frying pan, small and large saucepans with lids		
Oven tray – a small, deep tray can double up as a cake tin		
Chopping knives x 2		
Chopping board		
Tin opener		
Bottle opener		
Pizza cutter		
Wooden spoons/spatulas		
Kettle		
Toaster/toastie maker		
Potato/vegetable peeler		
Large sieve		
Potato masher		
Cheese grater		
Measuring jug		
Clingfilm		
Foil		
Weighing scales		
Small sealable plastic bags		
Plastic boxes with lids for storage		
Fruit bowl/mixing bowl		
Bag closers		
Kitchen scissors (easier than a knife for cutting up meat)		
Casserole/pie dish		
Oven gloves		
Hand-held blender e.g. for smoothies		
Air fryer		

KITCHEN CHECKLIST *continued*

	Got	Packed
Cleaning:		
Washing up liquid		
Kitchen surface spray		
Washing up gloves		
Scrubbing sponges/sponge on a stick for washing up		
Flat sponges for wiping surfaces		
Tea towels		
Kitchen roll – lots		
Bin liners		

BATHROOM CHECKLIST

	Got	Packed
Bath towels x 2		
Hand towels x 3		
Bath mat		
Hanging shower basket		
Cleaning:		
Bathroom spray cleaner		
Bleach		
Bathroom cleaning sponges/sponge on a stick (for the basin, bath/shower)		
Kitchen roll (for cleaning the toilet and floor)		
Washing up gloves (separate to the kitchen pair)		
Toilet rolls		
Mould and mildew remover spray		

4

Laundry

It's likely you'll make some mistakes when doing your laundry and some items will change colour, lose their shape or shrink. Hopefully, most of that can be avoided by following the advice below.

This advice is a general guide to laundry. You must check the labels of your laundry in case some items require special handling e.g. hand wash only, dry clean only. A handy guide illustrating the common laundry symbols is included at the end of this chapter.

Frequency

- Whenever dirty/smelly!

- After one use: underwear, T-shirts, sports wear

- After a few wears/uses: pyjamas, outer clothes, pillow cases, towels

- Weekly/fortnightly: bedding

Temperature

- It's recommended that towels, sheets, sportswear and underwear are washed at 60°C. You could, however, wash them at a lower temperature if you use bio laundry liquid (although not recommended for people with very sensitive skin or on certain materials – read the label)

- Most other items normally 40°C

- Some items will need to be washed at a delicate 30°C e.g. fine tops or woollen jumpers. You probably won't have many of these so you might want to share a delicate machine wash with a friend or just wash by hand

Cost & Paying for Laundry

Laundry costs add up. A load of washing can be £2.80 and using the dryer £1.40 = £4.20 per load.

- The machines in halls are usually industrial size so you can launder a bin-bag size amount in one go

- When not washing towels or bedding, you might not have much laundry so consider sharing a load – and the cost – with a friend or flatmate

- Some people use specially designed sheets that you add to a mixed load of laundry: they stop colour runs by absorbing dye particles from the wash water. This could save you money by allowing you to do mixed colour loads. Read the instructions before using

- To save money, you could avoid the drying cost and, instead, invest in a clothes airer. Some halls have drying rooms

Many university launderettes use cashless systems.

- If it's cashless, there may be an app and/or a reloadable card that you purchase from the university reception, launderette or retail outlet on the campus

- A laundry app might identify when your laundry cycle is finished, which machines are free or when the launderette is at its quietest

How To...

Sort Your Laundry

- Separate your laundry according to colour and wash temperature

- Shake out clothes e.g. straighten sleeves and trouser legs, un-ball socks

- Empty pockets

- Wash jeans and sweaters inside out

- Wash clothes with transfers/vinyl decoration inside out and don't tumble them

- Do up zips and buttons before washing so that clothes keep their shape

- Check symbols for washing instructions

Use a Washing Machine

- Have the correct coins/loaded laundry card/laundry app on your phone

- Before putting clothes in, spin the drum (where the clothes go) by hand and look inside to check no clothes have been left behind e.g. a stray sock. Otherwise they could discolour your laundry

- Check that items can be washed in a washing machine – check the washing symbol on the label (see the end of this chapter)

- Put clothes in one item at a time so they are loosely piled in the machine

- Leave a gap of at least 10cm (a fist) at the top. If you overfill the machine then the clothes won't be cleaned properly

- Add the detergent: read the recommended amount and either add to the detergent drawer (middle section or labelled II) or place the tablet on the top of the laundry and towards the back of the machine
    - Check what type of detergent is used at home. Non-bio laundry liquid might be a better option if you have sensitive skin e.g. eczema

- Shut the door firmly and select the correct setting – usually by temperature or fabric

- Check the machine has started – it might not start if the door hasn't shut properly

- Check the time to complete the wash on the display and return a few minutes before this time

- You could leave your clothes basket in front or on top of the machine so, if you're late back, the next person has somewhere to put your clean laundry

- If the door doesn't open immediately on finishing, wait 1–2 minutes and try again – some machines have that safety feature built in

- Take the clothes out and spin the drum by hand/check inside to make sure you've not left anything behind

Hand Wash

A few items might require hand-washing. Hopefully not too many.

- Dissolve detergent in warm (not hot) water

- Wearing washing up gloves, dunk the item(s) and let them soak in the water for a few minutes so the detergent can get to work. Gently knead the items especially those areas that touch the body most often or are obviously soiled

- Gently squeeze out the water from the item(s), let the dirty water drain away

- Rinse in clean, cool water three times

- You may need to wrap the item(s) in a clean towel to help remove the excess water and then shake out and lay flat to dry

Use a Tumble Dryer

- Have the correct coins/loaded laundry card/laundry app on your phone

- Always remove fluff from the tumble dryer filter before and after you've used the machine

- If it's a condenser dryer, pour away the collected water from the container before and after using

- Check that items can be tumbled – look for the drying symbol: a circle inside a square

- Shake clothes out before putting in the dryer

- You may want to use two dryers for two separate loads: one for smaller items such as underwear (not bras – don't tumble these), pyjamas, lightweight tops etc which take less time to dry, and another for bedding, towels and heavy items such as hoodies, which will take longer

- Shut the door firmly and select the correct setting – usually by temperature or time

- Check the machine has started – it might not start if the door hasn't shut properly

- Check the time to complete the dry on the display and return a few minutes before this time

- You could leave your clothes basket in front or on top of the machine so, if you're late back, the next person has somewhere to put your dry laundry

- At the end, check the machine is empty – look inside the drum

Iron

- Check the care symbol on the item's label to ensure it can be ironed and at what heat

- Turn the dial to the correct temperature and wait for the iron to heat up

- Lay the item on the ironing board and adjust it so it's flat
    - Where the material is layered, e.g. trousers or sleeves, ensure the material underneath is also flat

- Avoid ironing over buttons, zips, hems and seams

- You can reduce the likelihood of wrinkling – and therefore ironing – by:

- Not overstuffing the washing machine
- Taking your clothes out of the washing machine as soon as it's finished
- Shaking out your clothes and laying them flat on a clothes airer, or on hangers, to dry
- When they're dry, fold them away or hang them up

LAUNDRY CHECKLIST

	Got	Packed
Laundry detergent		
Laundry basket		
Clothes airer		
Radiator airer		
Clothes pegs for small items		
Laundry bag		

Key To Common Laundry Symbols

Wash

Wash at or below 40°C

Hand wash

Do not wash

Number inside the symbol = maximum wash temperature
Horizontal bars under the symbol: None = cotton = maximum wash and spin
One bar = synthetic = medium wash and spin
Two bars = silk or wool = delicate wash and spin

Dry

Tumble drying (low temperature)

Tumble drying (normal)

Do not tumble dry

Line dry

Dry flat

Drip dry

Iron

Iron at low temperature

Iron at medium temperature

Iron at high temperature

Do not iron

Professional Cleaning

Professional cleaning symbol

Do not dry clean

Letters inside the circle and horizontal lines under the symbol are instructions for the professional cleaner

5

Food & Drink

Try to eat and drink healthily: you'll look and feel better for it.

Amongst other things, what you eat and drink affects your body shape, skin, eyes, hair and teeth; your mood, energy levels and ability to study and socialise; your digestive system, your heart and other organs; your strength, stamina and bone density; your sleep; your immune system; and your body's ability to grow and repair itself. So it's pretty important to eat the right food and in the correct amounts.

What Constitutes A Healthy Diet?

Unless you have specific dietary requirements, a healthy diet should include the following food groups. The majority of this information is taken from the NHS Eatwell guidelines (there's a helpful illustration on p72).

- Carbohydrates – just under 40% of what you eat
  - E.g. potatoes, bread, rice, pasta, cereal
  - Choose wholegrain, higher fibre and low sugar options

- Carbs give you energy, they contain fibre (important for your digestive system), they contain vitamins and minerals, and they make you feel full

- Protein – just over 10% of what you eat
  - E.g. meat, fish, eggs, pulses, nuts
  - Pulses – such as beans, peas and lentils – are a good alternative to meat because they're lower in fat, higher in fibre and protein, and cost less than meat
  - Government guidelines are to have two portions of fish each week, one of which should be oily e.g. salmon or mackerel
  - If you're eating meat, choose lean cuts, take the skin off poultry and eat less red and processed meat such as bacon, ham and sausages
  - Protein is essential to grow and repair cells, contains vitamins and minerals and helps you stay fuller for longer

- Vegetables and fruit – 40% of what you eat
  - Eat a variety and at least five portions per day
  - Fresh, frozen, tinned, dried or juiced are all good
  - Juice and/or smoothies are high in sugar and should be limited to 150ml a day
  - Vegetables and fruit provide important vitamins and minerals to help your body work properly and stay healthy
  - They're also an excellent source of fibre and can help prevent constipation and other digestive problems

- Dairy/dairy alternatives – just under 10% of what you eat
  - You could add it throughout the day e.g. milk with cereal, tea and coffee; butter or spread on sandwiches or toast; yoghurt or cheese for dessert
  - Choose lower fat and lower sugar versions
  - Dairy and dairy alternatives are a great source of protein, some vitamins, calcium and help keep bones strong

- Oils and spreads – 1% of what you eat
  - Choose unsaturated oils and spreads in small quantities e.g. vegetable, olive, sunflower and rapeseed oil
  - Fats help the body absorb vitamins A, D and E, which contribute to healthy eyes, skin, bones and the immune system

- Drink 6 to 8 cups/glasses of fluid a day
  - Water quenches your thirst, is free and it's good for you
  - Unsweetened tea, fruit tea, coffee, semi-skimmed, 1% fat or skimmed milk are also healthy alternatives
  - If you don't drink enough fluid, you might find it difficult to concentrate or think clearly or you may become constipated

If you want to eat or drink something sugary, fatty or salty, have these foodstuffs less often and in small amounts.

Spoon Sizes In Recipes

Tsp = 5ml = 1 x teaspoon
Dsp = dessert spoon = 10ml = 2 x teaspoons
Tbsp = tablespoon = 15ml = 3 x teaspoons

Cooking – Some General Advice

Having to think about what to eat, food shopping, cooking and then doing the washing up afterwards is, for a lot of students, a challenge: from the mental energy it requires, to the cost, to how time-consuming it can be.

"Having to prepare meals when I'm tired."

"I cannot explain how much I hate food shopping. Being an adult and having independence is great until you realise you've got to think of meals you want to eat every day."

For others, it's a joy:

"I really enjoy cooking my own meals with fresh vegetables every night."

"The satisfaction you get when you've managed to cook something delicious, entirely by yourself, is absolutely unparalleled."

To make things easier:

- Look online or get your parents or friends to show you how to make dishes you like and that are healthy, quick and easy to prepare

- Make a meal at least two portions in size and put the spare portion(s) in the fridge or freezer. You'll then have a meal ready – as you won't have to cook from scratch again – which can be really helpful at the end of a tiring day. Doing this meal prepping can save you time and money

- Buy, prepare, cook and clear away a meal for a friend or flatmate once a week and get them to do the same for you = one less meal to organise

- Instead of ordering a takeaway – which is usually expensive and high in fat, salt and sugar – use a good quality, low sugar and low salt variety of pasta sauce, curry sauce or pesto as a speedy base for dishes

- It's really important for health to eat colourful (not just beige) food

  - Ideally have two different vegetables with every meal – you'll quickly get your 5 a day

  - If cooking your veg on the hob, use a small amount of water to just cover the vegetables. Stir at least once and don't boil the life out of them. Usually takes 5–7 minutes

- After touching raw fish or meat, wash your hands with soap and hot water and wash chopping boards/utensils with hot water and washing up liquid

- Follow the cooking instructions on packaging

- Set the timer on your oven/phone in case you get distracted and forget you're cooking

Do you know how to serve everything hot at the same time? Keeping it covered means it will stay hot for around 5-10 minutes. If you've boiled food, pour away the water so it doesn't continue to cook and put the lid back on the pan. Or put hot food on a warm plate then cover with foil

Storing Leftovers

Keep any untouched (never half eaten: this is full of bacteria) leftovers – they can be a welcome quick and easy next meal.

- Cool down leftovers in 1–2 hours. Put into a container, cover and put in the fridge or freezer. Eat leftovers from the fridge within 1–2 days

- Cover your food securely. It stops anything from the shelf above dropping onto it, it will prevent the food from drying out and, if the container is tilted or pushed over, the contents are less likely to spill

- Always empty food out of metal tins into plastic storage pots/bags

- If food is reheated, always make sure it's piping hot before serving

- Rice must be cooled within 1 hour, stored in the fridge, eaten within a day, re-heated only once and must be steaming hot all the way through before serving

Five Easy Meals

Each of these simple recipes makes two portions: one to eat and one to share or save. Check cooking times on packaging and adjust accordingly. Stir all pans at least once during cooking.

Spaghetti Bolognese with Salad

1. Boil a pan of water and add two portions of spaghetti
2. Prepare a salad
3. Pan fry 200g of minced beef until brown (this is important for flavour). When browned, pour any excess oil into a mug (when cooled, soak up with kitchen roll and throw away)
4. If you want extra flavour/bulk you could add chopped carrots, mushrooms, bacon, lentils (pre-cooked from a tin or packet for speed), garlic, herbs (e.g. oregano, basil), a squirt of ketchup or tomato puree, a stock cube, a bit of wine (any type)
5. Add pasta sauce to the meat and heat through; simmer for 5 minutes
6. Drain the pasta and grate some cheese
7. Serve the Bolognese with grated cheese, pasta and salad

You can transform the Bolognese – or the spare portion – into a Chilli con Carne by reheating with a small tin of spicy beans and serving with a dollop of cream cheese or crème fraiche or sour cream

Chicken Korma with Rice, Broccoli, Green Beans and Naan Bread

1. Boil a pan of water and add two portions of rice
2. Slice two breasts of chicken. Heat one teaspoon of oil in a frying pan and, when hot, add the chicken. Turn down the heat to medium and pan fry until lightly browned and no longer pink in the middle
3. Boil a second pan of water and add broccoli and green beans
4. Add korma sauce to the chicken and heat through
5. If you want extra flavour/bulk you could add a small tin of butter beans or chick peas, cashew nuts or a handful of raisins and heat through

6. Drain the rice, broccoli and green beans and lightly toast the naan
7. Serve the chicken korma with the rice, broccoli, green beans and naan

Pesto Pasta with Chicken, Peas and Sweetcorn

1. Boil a pan of water and add two portions of pasta
2. Slice two breasts of chicken. Heat 1 teaspoon of oil in a frying pain and, when hot, add the chicken. Turn down the heat to medium and pan fry until lightly browned and no longer pink in the middle
3. Add frozen peas and sweetcorn to the pasta and cook for 3–4 minutes
4. Drain the pasta, peas and sweetcorn, add the cooked chicken and two dessert spoons of pesto, stir through and serve

Pan Fried Salmon Fillet with Potatoes, Green Beans and Spinach

1. Boil a pan of water and add two portions of halved new potatoes
2. Wait 5 minutes then boil a second pan of water and, to this pan, add the green beans and spinach
3. Heat 1 teaspoon of oil in a frying pain and, when hot, add the salmon. Turn down the heat to medium, sprinkle a little salt and pepper over the fish and pan fry until it's cooked all the way through
4. Add 2 teaspoons of butter and 1 teaspoon of lemon juice to the pan and heat through
5. Drain the new potatoes, green beans and spinach and serve the salmon, butter and lemon sauce

Roasted Potatoes and Vegetables Topped with Crumbled Goats Cheese

1. Heat the oven to 180°C fan/200°C regular oven
2. In a bowl, make a marinade of 2 tablespoons of olive oil, 1 teaspoon of grainy mustard, 1 tablespoon of runny honey and salt and pepper
3. Wash and chop two sweet potatoes into the size of new potatoes or halve 10 new potatoes and put in a large oven tray (or do a mix of both). Add a selection of vegetables chopped into large pieces

e.g. peppers, courgette, aubergine, red onion, mushrooms, carrots, butternut squash, whole tomatoes, baby corn

4. Stir the marinade and pour over the vegetables; stir to ensure the vegetables are coated
5. Roast the vegetables in the middle of the oven (stirring half way) for about 30 minutes until the potatoes are soft
6. Serve the roasted vegetables with some goats cheese crumbled on top and sliced French bread on the side

Light Meal/Snack Ideas

Stuck for ideas? Try one of these:

- Toast/crumpets/bagels/sandwiches/wraps/pitta/crackers/rice cakes with: cheese and tomato, tuna mayo with sweetcorn or cucumber, salad and hummus, mashed avocado, cooked chicken and salad, scrambled egg, brie and cranberry, peanut butter, egg mayonnaise, smoked salmon and cream cheese
- Jacket potato with: curried chicken, grated cheese and baked beans, chilli, roasted vegetables, tuna mayo with sweetcorn
- Soup and a sandwich
- Cereal with fruit, nuts and/or seeds and milk
- Yoghurt – add fruit and muesli to make it more filling

Useful Resources

- The NHS Eatwell Guide, on p72, shows how much of what you eat overall should come from each food group

- There are some great recipe books available – some especially aimed at students – with tasty and easy-to-follow recipes that won't break the bank. You could also create your own recipe book with recipes from home, meal ideas from friends and suggestions found online

USEFUL SHOPPING LIST

PRODUCE		
Fruit		
Vegetables – frozen might last longer/be more economical		
Salad		
BAKERY		
E.g. bread/bagels/pitta/naan – most can be frozen if you have too much		
PACKETS/JARS/TINS/BOXES		
Rice/pasta/noodles		
Stir-in sauces for pasta/curry/stir fry		
Sauces e.g. soy, vinegar, ketchup, sweet chilli, mayonnaise, tomato puree		
Tinned tuna/other fish		
Tinned vegetables e.g. tomatoes, baked beans, lentils, beans, chickpeas		
Seasoning e.g. salt & pepper, stock cubes		
Dried herbs and spices e.g. basil, oregano, chilli, turmeric, curry, cumin		
Oil for cooking/dressings		
Breakfast cereal		
Eggs		
Toast/sandwich fillings e.g. jam, honey, Marmite, peanut butter		
Snacks to share e.g. biscuits, crisps, nuts, popcorn, chocolate		
Sugar		
DAIRY/CHILLED		
Milk/dairy alternative		
Butter/spread		
Cheese		
Yoghurt		
Hummus/other dips		
Meat/other e.g. chicken, mince (buy the best you can afford), fish, Quorn		
Pizza/ready meals – frozen is often cheaper		
DRINKS		
Tea, coffee, hot chocolate		
Fruit juice/squash		
Alcohol/non-alcoholic drink to celebrate & mixers		

Eatwell Guide

Use the Eatwell Guide to help you get a balance of healthier and more sustainable food.
It shows how much of what you eat overall should come from each food group.

Choose wholegrain or higher fibre versions with less added fat, salt and sugar

Potatoes, bread, rice, pasta and other starchy carbohydrates

Bagels

Rice

Whole wheat pasta

Spaghetti

Cous Cous

Porridge

Whole grain cereal

Potatoes

Eat at least 5 portions of a variety of fruit and vegetables every day

Fruit and vegetables

Raisins

Chopped tomatoes

Frozen peas

Dairy and alternatives

Choose lower fat and lower sugar options

Soya drink

Semi milk

Beans, pulses, fish, eggs, meat and other proteins

Eat more beans and pulses, 2 portions of sustainably sourced fish per week, one of which is oily. Eat less red and processed meat

Lentils

Lean mince

Beans lower salt and sugar

Tuna

Chick peas

Plain nuts

6-8 a day

Water, lower fat milk, sugar-free drinks including tea and coffee all count.

Limit fruit juice and smoothies to 150ml a day.

Oil & spreads

Choose unsaturated oils and use in small amounts

Per day | 2000kcal | 2500kcal = ALL FOOD + ALL DRINKS

Check the label on packaged foods

Each serving (150g) contains

Energy 1046kJ 250kcal	Fat 3.0g	Saturates 1.3g	Sugars 34g	Salt 0.9g
13%	4%	7%	38%	15%
	LOW	LOW	HIGH	MED

of an adult's reference intake
Typical values (as sold) per 100g: 697kJ/167kcal

Choose foods lower
in fat, salt and sugars

Eat less often and in small amounts

Crisps

Sauce

© Crown copyright 2016.

Source: Public Health England in association with the Welsh Government, Food Standards Scotland and the Food Standards Agency in Northern Ireland

6
Friendships & Relationships

Friendships

Many of you will have attended the same school or college for the last seven years: you know who everyone is and you know all their stories. Going to university is an opportunity to meet a bunch of new people. Most of them are likely to be around your age and many of them will have a similar outlook or interests to you.

One Of *The* Best Things About Being At University

In my research, meeting new people and making new friends was considered to be one of the best things about being at university. Plus, if you're living away from home, you're able to spend as much time as you like with these new friends:

"So many like-minded people around you!"

"Always having people my age around."

"Having the opportunity to speak to/meet new people from all over the country/world, as you never would've met them if you didn't go to uni."

"Moving to a new place and meeting new people is so, so exciting."

"Whilst the studying is great, and I love my course, the best moments often come at 2 or 3 in the morning on a Friday night when you're sat with your flatmates laughing and joking about random things."

Finding And Making New Friends

It's common for new students to feel some anxiety about finding and making new friends but try not to worry. Most students tend to arrive at the same time, many of them won't know anyone else either, they're probably feeling the same way as you and most will want to make friends.

There are lots of opportunities to meet people.

- Even before you arrive, you can start the process by looking for the university's social media sites dedicated to its new students. Read Chapter 2: Important Things To Do Before The Start Of Term

- If you're moving to university, your flatmates are likely to be the first people you meet
    - You might have a shared kitchen or lounge: if you hear people are in it, take a deep breath, put on a big smile and go and say hello
    - Take a pack of cards or a game to play with your new flatmates on the first night – you can get to know each other whilst you're playing a game
    - Take a doorstop to prop your door open when you're in – it shows you're welcoming. And keep a packet of biscuits in your room to share with anyone who drops by

- Be proactive at getting along with your flatmates e.g. offer to make them tea and coffee; offer to walk to the university, bar or library; take in packages for each other; agree house rules (and try and stick to them); eat your meals in the shared area not in your room

"Get to know your flatmates well, as having a good relationship with them makes a big difference."

"I sat in my room for the first few nights but then I thought I need to get out and engage. I forced myself out and, before I knew it, I was having a great time chatting to everyone."

- And if you don't gel with your flatmates, don't worry. You have plenty of other ways to find your people

- You'll see the people on your course regularly and you already have a subject interest in common
  - If you're on a course where there are hundreds of other people in your lectures then it might feel difficult to talk to anyone. But we're creatures of habit and we often sit in the same place so you're likely to start recognising the same faces. Smile and say hello
  - Seminars and tutorials should start in weeks 2 or 3. You'll be in smaller groups and you'll start to recognise the same people each week, which will make it easier to talk to each other
  - And you could create, or join, study groups so you can talk about the course and build friendships with each other

"Introduce yourself to everyone you meet or sit next to in lectures because you never know who will turn out to be your good friends."

"Find and make friends with people on your course. It's good as you can support each other and help develop a better understanding of content between you."

- Join societies and clubs that you have a genuine interest in
  - This is a great way to make friends as you have common interests, which gives you something to talk about/do together
  - If you're focused on something, you're less likely to experience awkward silences
  - And you can even join a club just for the socials

"Try everything, even if you're only slightly interested in it. It could lead to making friends, or just people to talk to before you find 'your people'. And at the very least it could be something to joke about later – you can always drop it if you don't enjoy it."

"Always join a society. Good idea if you don't get along with your flat, you have the opportunity to make friends elsewhere."

"Join societies. There's always some out there for you. I struggle loads with people, hate clubbing and drinking, and have managed to make plenty of friends through societies."

"Join as many societies/group chats as possible. Even if you don't play the sport, you can still go out on student nights with them and it's a great way to meet new people."

- You're likely to be in many, many queues – from getting your room key to lining up for food, standing at a bar to waiting outside a classroom. Smile and say hello to the person standing next to you

- And be yourself at university. Don't pretend to be someone you're not. University is a great place to be your authentic self and you're more likely to find people who are similar to you and who will like you for who you are

"No one is going to judge you or look at you funny because we're all students. We're all in the same boat. At the end of the day, we don't know

anything about each other when we all first meet so be true to yourself."

"Always remember no one is going to judge you and this time of your life isn't going to come back so follow your heart and live your life!!!"

"Just be yourself and do not worry about what others are doing. Do whatever you enjoy and what makes you happy."

Realistically it could be awkward but talking to everyone and being open to making friends was a recurring piece of advice from the first year students in my research:

"Don't feel shy, literally everyone wants to make friends and is in the same boat."

"Embrace everything and fake confidence until you make it."

"Don't be afraid to say hello to new people! It's daunting at first but you'll never find your people if you don't try! Everyone is in the same boat so step out of your comfort zone and introduce yourself :)"

"Just try and be confident and talk to anyone at first. Everyone wants to make friends but some people are more scared. But if you act confident and friendly, people are immediately attracted to you. Ask questions, people love to talk about themselves and don't be scared to ask for socials to keep in touch. There's a one month period where it's fully normal to talk to anyone you meet, anywhere at uni."

And there are lots of things you can do to help smooth things along, for example:

- Topics of conversation – you can initiate it: where they're from, what they're studying, where they're living, what clubs or societies they're joining or interests they have. The weather

- Offer to make your flatmates a cup of tea or coffee, or go to a cafe with your course mates during breaks in classes

- Offer to walk together e.g. to class, to a club, to the library, to the supermarket, to a bar

- And smile at people. When we're nervous or anxious we often look away too quickly after smiling at people in case they don't return a smile. Wait a second longer before you turn away since they might not have been expecting to see a friendly face

Freshers' Week

The first week you arrive at university is generally known as Freshers' (or Welcome) Week. This is the time when the Students' Union puts on social, sporting and interest events and the university welcomes you.

- Do attend different events and society meetings that appeal to you: you can try out new activities, continue with interests you already have and it's a great way to make friends as you're meeting people similar to you

- You don't have to commit to a club straight away – you can normally attend a trial session

- Don't feel under pressure to go to clubs and bars and drink alcohol during Freshers' Week if that's not your thing. There are an increasing number of fun 'Sober Socials' – events that don't involve alcohol and nightclubs – in response to a growing number of students wanting to attend alcohol-free get-togethers

Don't Panic

The first few weeks at university aren't the only time you'll get to meet people, so don't worry if you don't find your close friends straightaway.

- Although some great friendships can be made in the first few weeks, you'll be meeting new and interesting people throughout your entire time at university e.g. through societies, taking different course modules, through other people

"You won't meet all of your uni friends during Freshers' Week so try not to stress too much about it."

"It's never 'too late' to make friends. Don't worry if you struggle to find your people in Freshers' Week, you'll meet new people all year."

"Freshers is really overhyped so don't stress about it. You will make friends. For some it takes more time than others but you will find them. Just be open to talking to others regardless of accommodation or course. Everyone calms down by week six and you go out when, and with who, you want."

"Don't worry if you don't find people you're really close to in the first term. People are thrown together and you may only get on really well with a couple to start with – and that's okay. Just be sociable and you'll be alright."

- Also, you don't have to stay attached to the first friendly person you meet – unless you want to

- If you're feeling a bit lonely, sad or homesick, read Chapter 9
  - You'll see that you're not alone and, for most students, over time you'll become more settled and things will get better

- And a number of Freshers, in my research, made thoughtful comments, including:

"Everyone doesn't feel fully prepared for university and that's ok."

"Don't worry if you don't instantly find your people, you will find friends."

"It'll take you some time to ease in and get used to everything and that's okay. Everyone gets adjusted at a different pace so try not to compare yourself to others."

"There will be people who like you, always"

I Know We've Only Just Met But Shall We Live Together?

It's becoming increasingly common for first year students to organise accommodation for their second year in the first term of their first year.

- This means that you might find yourself committing to living with people – in a year's time and for an academic year – who you've only known for a couple of months!

- You can choose to do this or not. You just need to weigh up whether you feel more comfortable having this organised ahead of time – even if it means your flatmates might not turn out to be your close friends – or whether you'd be happy to sort out your accommodation at a later date

- It might be reassuring to know:
  - Student accommodation is often located in neighbouring areas so you'll probably be living near your close friends even if you don't live with them
  - Sometimes you can really like someone but find them impossible to live with so it's not always best to live with your friends
  - When you share a home you get to know people well so you might develop unexpected friendships with your new housemates

- It's also worth bearing in mind that committing to your second year's accommodation early on means you'll need to pay a month's deposit within weeks of handing over your first year's deposit. Given the cost of accommodation, you might need access to c.£500–1,000, which will be tied up in your first and second years' accommodation deposits

- You should also be aware that, if it's student housing you're renting, it's common practice to take over the tenancy from the date the current students vacate the property. So, even if you're not moving in until September/October, you may be paying rent and bills from July

- Your university accommodation department may offer a contract-checking service or advice on housing regulations in the private sector

- And, if you choose not to commit in that first term of starting university, really don't worry. You'll still find somewhere to live and people to live with in a year's time. For example:
    - It's not uncommon for friendships or circumstances to change over the course of a year and someone who committed early on to a house might decide against it at a later date – leaving a room needing to be filled. You see spare rooms, in student houses, posted on Facebook and other social sites, all year round
    - You may find that, if available, living in a hall of residence suits you in your second year

And you may not have to move out of university accommodation at all. Students at some, particularly collegiate, universities may be able to stay living in their college accommodation for a further year or two.

Relationships, Sex & Intimacy

(Did the book fall open at this page?)

There are likely to be thousands of people, many the same age as you, at your university. Amongst all of those people, it's likely there will be some who you're attracted to.

Just like you, they're bright, they're excited to be there, they're keen to meet other people, many of them will have the same interests and outlook as you, lots of them are living away from home for the first time and they're experiencing complete freedom to do what they like and date whoever they fancy. With all that power comes responsibility.

Questions To Ask Yourself

Prior to embarking on any intimacy, ask yourself:

- Would you still fancy that person in the cold light of day?

- Would it be awkward or lovely to see them again?

- Would you still be their cup of tea tomorrow? You'll have an idea of this if you know them already

- Do they treat you well every time you see them? Are they excited to see you? Do they introduce you to their friends?

- Do you feel you're being pressured into intimacy or having sex? Perhaps to keep your partner or to impress other people?
    - Don't ever feel pressured into any form of intimacy or having sex

- Are you putting pressure on someone to be intimate with you?
    - If you're struggling with the issue of consent just imagine that, instead of initiating sex, you're making someone a cup of tea. Take a look at this excellent video, Tea Consent, which explains what consent is when it comes to sexual interactions: https://www.youtube.com/watch?v=fGoWLWS4-kU

And remember that:

- Intimacy and sex are expressions of love and you or your partner might wish to wait a significant period of time or until a long-term commitment has been made

- Intimacy and sex aren't the only aspects of a relationship, and there are other ways of enjoying each other's company

Advice On Intimacy

If you decide to be intimate with someone:

- Prior to entering into a sexual relationship, consider being tested for STIs (sexually transmitted infections)

- Use a condom. Condoms help reduce the spread of STIs. These infections include HIV (Human Immunodeficiency Virus), chlamydia, genital herpes, genital warts, gonorrhoea, hepatitis B, and syphilis

- To prevent an unintended pregnancy, you should use another form of contraception in addition to a condom

- If you're certain that you want to be intimate with someone: be respectful, be clean, be kind, use contraception and be enthusiastic!

- If you've had unprotected sex or your contraception fails:
    - Emergency contraception can prevent pregnancy
    - There are currently two types of emergency contraception: the emergency contraceptive pill (the 'morning after' pill) and the intrauterine device (IUD or coil)
    - Don't delay in seeking emergency contraception: the sooner you use it, the more effective it will be
    - You can get emergency contraception for free from a variety of centres including contraception clinics, some GP surgeries and most pharmacies (and some of those pharmacies can be found in supermarkets), but they may not all fit the IUD
    - For more information, go to https://www.nhs.uk/conditions/contraception/emergency-contraception/

- If you regret being intimate with someone:
  - Don't be too hard on yourself. We all make mistakes and the thing to do is learn from those mistakes and move on a little wiser
  - Put it down to experience, acknowledge you've learned a lesson and try not to let it happen again

Existing Relationships

Perhaps you're already in a relationship with someone. If you're moving away then it might feel very hard to leave them.

- Do throw yourself into university life: go to Freshers' Week and make friends, join clubs and societies, meet your flatmates and find the students on your course. These are the people who you'll be with on a day-to-day basis – some for the next three to four years – and they often end up being friends for life

- It might feel a bit hard to keep a relationship going when there's so much going on in your new life – but it's certainly possible

- If your partner has also gone to university then that could be helpful as you'll both have an understanding of each other's daily lives and can share experiences

- If your partner hasn't gone to university, then they might find it difficult to imagine your new life and might even feel a bit threatened by you striking out on your own and how busy and exciting your new life appears to be

- If you're able, invite them to visit. Keep speaking and texting so they feel involved and can picture you in, and continue to be part of, your new life

7

Money: Where It Goes & How To Get More Of It

One of the most important things you learn as a student is how to budget and how to live on a restricted income. Not having enough money, however, is a common complaint – and worry – amongst students.

Where It Goes

Assuming you know how much money you'll have at the beginning of each term then you need to allocate your money to the following areas:

- Rent – this is likely to be your biggest outgoing

- Groceries – these may be included if you're in a catered hall but not every meal may be provided or you may want to eat elsewhere occasionally

- Household bills e.g. gas, electricity, water, phone/broadband. These may be included if you're in halls or in some rental properties but you must check and allocate your money accordingly

- Going out e.g. pubs/bars, nightclubs, cinema, gigs

- Transport – to university/work/going out/going home. Usually by public transport but may include the occasional taxi. Discount rail and coach cards are a good idea

- Takeaways and eating out

- Clothes and shopping

- Holidays and events

- Health and wellbeing – this could include club memberships, subs, equipment, kit, travel, entry into pool, gym etc

- Mobile phone – if you're out of contract and happy with your phone, there are some great SIM-only deals available

- Course materials e.g. books, kit, equipment, uniform, printing, membership, field trips

- Gifts and charity

- Friends and family

- Other – there are ALWAYS extras or unexpected items

BUDGET TABLE

	Amount per TERM (£)
Rent	
Groceries	
Household bills	
Going out	
Transport	
Takeaways and eating out	
Clothes and shopping	
Holidays and events	
Health and wellbeing	
Mobile phone	
Course materials	
Gifts and charity	
Friends and family	
Extras	
TOTAL	£
Total amount of money you have at the start of each TERM	£
Minus Total above	£
Leaves you with…	£

Rent

If you're living away from home, rent is usually your biggest expenditure.

- If you pay each term's rent up-front, then you'll know what you have left for everything else

- Save the Student, the student money website, carries out an annual National Student Money Survey. It has some particularly useful tables on its website that show average student living costs and also average rent at each university around the country. Take a look at this link:
  - https://www.savethestudent.org/money/student-budgeting/what-do-students-spend-their-money-on.html

Accommodation deposits

If you're living away from home, a very large additional item is your accommodation deposit: it could be one month's rent.

- It's becoming increasingly common for students to organise their accommodation for their second year in the first term of their first year. This means that, within a matter of weeks of paying up to a month's deposit for your first year's accommodation, you could be paying another month's deposit for your second year's accommodation

- Realistically, given the cost of accommodation, you may need to be able to access c.£500–1,000, which will be tied up in the two deposits

Healthcare Costs

If you're a UK resident then you're probably used to most medical treatment being free (at the point of delivery) under the NHS. When you become 19, however, if you're registered with a GP in England, you'll normally have to start paying for some elements of your healthcare e.g. prescriptions.

There are ways that you might be able to reduce these costs, for example:

- If you're on a low income, you might qualify for free or discounted medical costs. How much help you get depends on your weekly income and necessary outgoings, plus any savings or investments you have at the time you apply. Search the NHS Low Income Scheme

- If you're over the financial threshold and you need regular prescriptions, you can pay a set price for three or twelve months, no matter how many you need. Search NHS Prescription Prepayment Certificate

If you're registered with a GP in Scotland, Wales or Northern Ireland then prescriptions are currently free from a pharmacist in those countries.

Tuition Fees

The tuition fee is set by your university. If you're eligible, and you require it, you can apply to the UK government for a tuition fee loan. See p90 for the UK government student finance websites.

- These loans are paid directly to the university from the student finance company (therefore you won't need to allocate money for tuition in your termly budget)

- The value of the tuition fee loan varies depending on factors such as:
  - Whether the course is full- or part-time
  - Where in the UK the university is located
  - Where you're from
  - Whether you're on a placement year or studying abroad
  - Whether you're studying for an accelerated degree (see p100 for more information)

- If you live in Scotland and decide to study at a university in Scotland, you currently won't have to pay anything towards tuition fees (criteria apply)

How To Support Yourself Whilst Studying

Maintenance Loan

If you're eligible, and you require it, you can apply to the UK government for a maintenance loan to go towards living costs.

- How much maintenance loan you get depends on various factors such as:
  - Where you're from
  - Where you're studying
  - Your household income
  - Whether you're living at home or not
  - Whether you're studying full- or part-time

- Maintenance loans are paid directly into your bank account, in three instalments, usually at the start of each term (monthly if studying in Scotland)

Follow this link for a handy student finance calculator for students from England or the EU starting a new undergraduate course. It estimates student loans and extra state funding. The results are more accurate if you know your annual household income (your parents' or partner's income plus your own):

- www.gov.uk/student-finance-calculator

Follow these links for information on student loans:

- England: www.gov.uk/student-finance
- Scotland: www.saas.gov.uk
- Wales: www.studentfinancewales.co.uk
- Northern Ireland: www.studentfinanceni.co.uk
- Jersey: https://www.gov.je/working/careers/16to19yearolds/enteringhighereducation/financinghighereducationcourses/Pages/index.aspx
- Guernsey: https://www.gov.gg/studentfinance
- Isle of Man: https://www.gov.im/student-grants

The amount of maintenance loan you receive may not be sufficient to even pay your rent. You must therefore find other ways to make ends meet

Government Grants/Allowances

You may be eligible for additional financial support in the form of government grants or allowances, which you can apply for when you apply for student loans.

- They're available to meet a range of needs, for example if you:
  - Are under 25, have no contact with your parents and support yourself (and if you are a care leaver, check with your university as it may offer year-round accommodation)
  - Pay for childcare
  - Are a full-time student with children
  - Have an adult who depends on you financially
  - Have a disability, mental or physical health problem or learning difficulty, like dyslexia
  - Are on a low income
  - Are a medical, social work or a teacher training student
  - Are studying abroad – you might get a grant to cover some travel expenses

Your Family

Your family – possibly parents or grandparents – may be in a position to support you in some way.

- You should discuss this with them in advance so you know whether and how much money they're able to give you and how often you'll receive that money. You may find budgeting easier if they transfer money to you on a weekly basis

- The amount you receive in the maintenance loan is partly based on family income therefore this does imply that your parents are expected to help you financially, where they're able

- As a guide, you could ask your parents to make up the shortfall between the amount in maintenance loan that you receive and the maximum maintenance loan
  - For example, if the maximum maintenance loan for a full-time undergraduate student from England, living away from home and outside London is £9,500 but you only receive £6,500 in

maintenance loan, then you could ask your parents to contribute £3,000 per year towards your living costs

- If they're able to contribute more this would be helpful since many students find it difficult to keep within the maximum maintenance loan (especially given the cost of rent)

- It's possible, however, that your family isn't able to contribute towards your living costs

Savings

Try and build up your savings, e.g. from part-time jobs and gifts, before you leave for university so you have money to fall back on whilst you're waiting for your next instalment of funding.

Scholarships, Bursaries, Grants & Awards

According to The Scholarship Hub, which helps students find alternative sources of funding, millions of pounds in the form of grants, bursaries and scholarships, are available to UK students each year – yet organisations often struggle to attract enough applicants. Your chances of being successful, if you apply, are therefore greater than you might think.

There are a number of useful resources where you can search for funding to see whether you qualify, how much you could get and how to apply.

- Universities
    - Websites: search under scholarships, grants, awards and bursaries
    - At Open Days: attend the finance talk to hear what they have to say about alternative sources of funding
    - Student finance department: talk to them directly as they might know of pots of money that haven't yet been listed on the university website

- Useful websites that have assembled the details of a huge number of trusts, foundations, etc include:
  - The Scholarship Hub: www.thescholarshiphub.org.uk
  - Turn2us is a national charity that helps people in financial hardship gain access to welfare benefits, charitable grants and support services www.turn2us.org.uk

- Look for The Guide to Educational Grants

- The time to apply varies – don't panic if you've already started a course
  - Some organisations invite applications whilst you're studying for A levels or when you have your university place confirmed, some stipulate that you should be in your first or subsequent years, and others are only available on graduation

- Start looking early so you can identify deadlines and have sufficient time to gather your evidence and prepare your application

- Unlike other student finance, this type of funding doesn't normally have to be paid back

- Funding is available for a wide variety of applicants. For example:
  - Students who are from a disadvantaged background or in severe financial need
  - Students whose academic performance, sporting or musical achievements are excellent; the funding is often to help you keep up these activities
  - If you're studying a specific course or subject
  - Based on where you live or where you're from. If you've moved away to go to uni, this doubles your opportunities: you can apply based on your university town and your home town
  - Based on what your family does for a living or who you're descended from
  - If you need to travel for your course or study or work abroad

- If you have a disability or if you have dependents who rely on you
- Funding is also available for a whole host of other reasons and some are quite unusual e.g. if you're a vegetarian or if you're entrepreneurial

You might think that spending a few hours searching for funding and then writing a letter or filling in an application form is a faff. However, if you get paid around £6/hour doing a Saturday job, you'll earn about £40-50 in a day; it would therefore take you around three months to earn the same as a £600 award

Part-Time Paid Work

Consider working part-time. You won't be alone: research shows that around three quarters of students work part-time to help fund their studies.

During term-time you could consider:

- University jobs: look for jobs within departments, the library, the Student Union or as a student ambassador (helping prospective students and their families at Open Days or helping new students at moving-in days)

- Jobs in pubs, cafes or restaurants often come with the added bonus that you get fed too

- Jobs in department stores often give decent staff discounts and you can use it across all the different departments e.g. clothes, shoes, sportswear

- Do you have a skill you can sell? E.g. artwork; sports coaching; academic or music tutoring

If you want to do paid work during the holidays:

- Let previous employers know when you're home and that you'll be happy to work for them

- Look for Christmas jobs well in advance

Try not to rely on a part-time job as your main source of income to fund your living costs. It's unlikely that you'll earn enough money to support yourself and working long shifts will impact your studies. Plus it would leave you with little time to socialise or relax, which is an important part of university life and crucial for your mental health.

If you're an international student, find out whether you're allowed to undertake paid work and, if so, how many hours you're allowed to do.

Fee Waivers

A university might offer a fee waiver – where the university pays part or all of a student's tuition fee.

- Check your university website for criteria e.g. it might be available to those on a low income or students showing exceptional talent

Hardship Funds

You could get emergency cash from your university if you're experiencing financial hardship and are at risk of dropping out. Contact your university student services department to find out if you're eligible.

- You'll need to provide evidence and they're unlikely to help if it's simply a case of over-spending

- It's often a once-only payment

Bank Overdraft

You might have opted for a student bank account, which normally has fee-free and interest-free overdraft facilities.

- Try only to go into the overdraft facility of your bank account as an emergency

- Try to avoid going over your overdraft limit as you'll incur additional charges and fees

- Remember, an overdraft is a loan: whatever you borrow has to be paid back. And its rate will increase once you graduate

Emergency Money

Keep £20 in a safe place that you carry on you e.g. in your phone case. Do not touch it. It's there for emergencies e.g. if you lose your purse/wallet or you run out of money or you need to get a taxi home. If you must use it, replace it.

Shop Savvy

You may now be buying some, if not all, of your food, personal and household requirements. Given that you're likely to be on a restricted income, there are some things you should bear in mind.

Before You Go Shopping

- Check your cupboards in advance and write a shopping list – this avoids possible throwing away or having to store duplicate purchases

- Take your own reusable shopping bags otherwise you're likely to be charged for a bag

- Eat before you go food shopping – it really cuts down on impulse buying

- Keep your receipts in case you need to return or exchange something

- Where possible, use cash rather than a debit or credit card – you're more likely to keep track of your spending

Where to Shop

- It's usually cheaper to buy from a supermarket rather than from a corner or campus shop
  - And look on price comparison sites: some supermarkets routinely feature as being cheaper than others

What to Buy

- Branded items are usually more expensive
  - You should ask yourself if you can tell the difference between the branded and the own-brand version
  - If you can, or if it's important, then go ahead but cut back on your spending somewhere else

- When looking at the cost of items, check the shelf label for the cost per volume e.g. 100g/kg/sheets/tablets etc – not the pack price – and compare that with the alternatives on the shelf. Huge savings can be made. For example, 100 sheets of a branded kitchen roll can be a whopping three times the cost of the store brand version

- Frozen vegetables might be a good idea since you won't have to eat them straightaway and they'll last longer than fresh vegetables

- Try to buy fruits and vegetables that are in season: they're normally cheaper and taste better

- Meat and fish can be the most expensive food ingredients on a shopping list whereas pulses – such as beans, lentils and peas – are some of the cheapest
  - Pulses are low in calories and fat but packed with fibre, vitamins and minerals
  - Use them in dishes to replace some or all of the meat e.g. kidney beans in chilli con carne or chickpeas in a chicken curry
  - Try a few vegetarian meals during the week to keep costs down. Thousands of people regularly take part in meat-free Monday

- It's often cheaper to buy items loose rather than already bagged e.g. fruit and vegetables. And you get to check them for bruises etc

- Avoid pre-sliced or prepared items as the more that's done for you, the more you normally pay

- Look for BOGOF: buy one get one free – maybe you can store or freeze the spare

Deal or Not Such a Good Deal

- Look out for deals/special offers – but always check the price per volume

- It helps to have an idea of what things normally cost so you know if something's really a good deal

- Discount stores might be selling something for £1 but it could be a smaller size and therefore more expensive by volume than the regular sized item from elsewhere

When to Buy

- It's often cheaper to buy fresh items at the end of the day when they've been marked down (often identified by their yellow label)

- However, choice will be limited, check for any damage and be sure you'll eat it (or freeze it) before it goes off

Discount Deals

There are a variety of discount deals you could use, for example:

- You could save money on travel by investing in a discount card e.g. 16–25 Railcard, Young Persons Coachcard
  - And you can normally save money on travel tickets by booking train and coach fares in advance

- Discount providers allow you to access a host of savings and many are aimed specifically at students.

Download student discount apps e.g UNiDAYS, Student Beans, TOTUM – they're specifically aimed at students and tend to offer discounts on relevant products

- Sign up for discount/loyalty cards where you normally shop e.g. supermarkets or chemists. They often give you money-off vouchers or discounts

- If eating out, look online for 2-for-1 deals

- Offer to be a model/have your hair cut by a trainee at a salon. An experienced hairdresser normally oversees but you pay a discounted price

Save Money: Alternatives To The Typical Degree

There are a number of different ways you can obtain a university degree and the following will cost you less than if you were to follow the traditional three-year, full-time route.

Accelerated Degree

Accelerated degree courses result in the same qualification as traditional undergraduate honours degree courses and normally have the same curriculum and content. However:

- An accelerated course is compressed – the most common scenario is a degree course delivered in two years instead of three

- This accelerated delivery is usually achieved by having shorter or fewer academic breaks during the year e.g. by running the course through the summer

- If you opt to study for an accelerated degree, you could:
    - Save 20 per cent on tuition fees compared to a traditional course (studying at a public university)
    - Have one year less maintenance costs
    - Start your career sooner

- Check online to see which universities and what courses are being offered under the accelerated option

Degree Apprenticeship

Degree apprenticeships have been developed by employers, universities and professional bodies working in partnership. If you opt for a degree apprenticeship you'd be employed by an organisation whilst studying for a degree on a part-time basis.

- You might attend university on a day-to-day schedule or in blocks of time, depending on the programme and the requirements of your employer

- The benefits of undertaking a degree apprenticeship include:
    - No tuition fee
    - No maintenance loan
    - You'd gain a degree and work experience
    - You'd be employed, trained and paid
    - And there's the likelihood of a permanent position on completion

- Degree apprenticeships can take between three to six years to complete, depending on the course level

- For more information and an up-to-date list of degree apprenticeships:
    - https://www.gov.uk/government/publications/higher-and-degree-apprenticeships

Sponsored Degree

- Students who are sponsored by an organisation may receive a salary or a bursary throughout their degree

- The sponsor may pay some or all of their tuition fees

- Students normally attend university on a full-time basis but undertake paid work for their sponsor during university holidays

- They're likely to be offered – or may be expected to take up – a role within the organisation on graduation

These schemes are pretty competitive so keep an eye on application deadlines. They're more common in certain sectors e.g. finance and business, technology, engineering and the military.

Money Difficulties – Do Not Panic

If you find yourself getting into difficulties with money, speak to:

- Your university student finance/student services department – you may be able to get additional income through grants or the hardship fund

- The bank

- Your parents, grandparents or other family members

- Read through the Scholarships, Bursaries, Grants & Awards section

Don't take out loans without getting advice from your university student finance department. Some loan companies charge phenomenal amounts of interest and you may end up with a bad credit rating – or worse – if you're unable to pay back the required amounts on time.

Repaying Government Loans

For many students, taking out the tuition fee loan and/or the maintenance loan for every year of your studies is a sobering thought. On paper, this looks like a significant amount of money: tuition fee and maintenance loans combined can amount to borrowings in the region of £50,000+.

However, it's important to remember that, the way repayments currently work, many students will re-pay only a small amount of what they owe and some will re-pay nothing at all.

For most undergraduate students, with a Plan 5 student loan, the following currently applies:

- Repayments don't start until April, the year after you graduate

- You only start repayments once you're earning above a certain salary threshold
  - So if you earn less than this, you won't repay anything towards your loans

- The amount you pay back is a percentage of the income you earn over the salary threshold. For example, if the salary threshold is £25,000 and the percentage to pay back is 9%:
  - If you earn £27,000 a year then you are £2,000 over the threshold
  - 9% of £2,000 is £180 a year so you will pay £15 each month towards your student loans
  - If you dip below £25,000 then repayments will stop

- If you're an employee then repayments are automatically made through the tax system

- Plan 5 repayments will stop if you have paid off your loan, are normally written off after forty years, or if you become permanently disabled or die

- For more information, read the guidance on repaying loans provided by your loan provider

These are useful resources for everything concerning student finance:

- https://www.gov.uk/browse/education/student-finance

- Save the Student: https://www.savethestudent.org

"Don't feel pressurized into anything, like you have to do what others are doing, as you don't. You do you."

8

Staying Safe At University

Keeping You & Your Belongings Safe

There are lots of things you can do to keep yourself and your belongings safe whilst you're at university. For example:

- Use locks and keys:
    - Use lock codes on all your devices e.g. on your phone and computer
    - Close entry doors behind you when you enter residential buildings
    - Don't allow people into residential buildings unless you know them
    - Lock your home's doors and windows securely when you leave
    - If you have a bike, lock it securely when not in use – even if it's inside your home

- Insure your belongings

- Back up your devices in case they're lost or stolen

- Put away sensitive information/important documents e.g. driving licence, bank card, bank statements

Staying Safe On Nights Out

- Make sure your phone is fully charged before you go out
- Have the telephone number of a reputable taxi firm in your phone
- Try not to withdraw cash from machines at night
- Keep your phone in your front pocket or, if it's in a bag, zip up your bag to reduce the chance of it being stolen
- Keep your drink covered (with your hand or a cover) to avoid the possibility of it being spiked
- Make plans in advance to go home with someone you trust
- Look out for each other: travel with your friends rather than on your own and agree no one is left alone or behind, especially if they're drunk
- If you are travelling or going somewhere alone, share your ETA or your location with a friend
- If travelling on public transport, sit near the driver or sit in a busy carriage. If you feel uncomfortable, move
- Don't take short cuts through quiet or dodgy areas – it's better to take the brighter, well-lit, busier route even if takes you a bit longer
- Tell the bar staff if you see anyone who looks like they're in an uncomfortable situation or losing control

Alcohol

Alcohol tends to be a big part of university life – especially when you first arrive – and there may be a drinking culture at the university or within some clubs and societies.

- You might experience pressure to drink – from people around you or from yourself – so that you feel you fit in. It's important to remember that it's okay not to drink to excess or not to drink at all

- If you're a non-drinker, you're not alone: a survey by the National Union of Students found that 21% of students don't drink alcohol

- And, in order to meet the increased demand amongst low or non-drinking students, the number of alcohol-free events (sometimes known as Sober Socials) run by universities, student unions and clubs and societies are increasing, as are alcohol-free student halls

Impact Of Alcohol

A person who has a normal tolerance for alcohol might find, after drinking one or two units, they feel warm, sociable and talkative.

However, more than that can have a variety of negative effects, such as:

- Your judgment and reasoning are affected, so you might lose self-control, become reckless, uninhibited or put yourself in a risky situation

- It can make you feel light headed, it can impair your memory, and reaction times and coordination can be affected

- It can affect your balance, make you slur or vomit – none of which is a good look

- Alcohol irritates your digestive system and can cause stomach pain, vomiting and diarrhoea

- It can make you vulnerable and there are people who'll take advantage of this e.g. they might steal your stuff, hurt you or be intimate with you without your consent

- If you're feeling low or stressed, you may be tempted to drink more alcohol – but alcohol is a depressant so any feelings can be worsened. And an underlying mental health disorder may also be worsened by alcohol use

- Too much too often can lead to a red, puffy face and a bloated stomach

- Your sleep is impacted: you'll get fewer hours of deep sleep, alcohol's a diuretic so your sleep will be disturbed as you'll need to go to the loo in the night, and you'll lose fluid through sweat so you'll be dehydrated. All in all, you'll wake feeling tired and groggy the next day

You're Not Drinking?

There are a number of good reasons for not drinking alcohol. If you feel that you need to explain why you're not drinking, you could say:

- You don't like the taste of it

- You don't like how it makes you feel

- For cultural reasons

- For health reasons e.g. a medication you're on is affected by alcohol

- You're sporty or health conscious. Alcohol is made from sugar or starch so it's full of 'empty' calories i.e. they have no nutritional value

- You have a sports event, deadline or early morning lecture so you need a clear head the next day

- It's too expensive

Whatever reason you have it's perfectly fine not to drink much or any alcohol. Over time, you should find that people will accept you as you are. You'll probably drift towards alcohol-free events and befriend other non-drinkers.

Initiations

Some clubs and societies encourage excessive drinking – usually followed by humiliating rituals – amongst new members at initiations.

Some people think it's a laugh but some people are scared of initiations – of the volume of alcohol they know they'll be expected to consume and the actions they'll be expected to perform.

There have been a number of deaths associated with initiations including that of Ed Farmer, a Newcastle University student who died after an Agricultural Society initiation in 2016. Ed was found at 4am, collapsed in the corridor of a student house, five times over the legal alcohol limit, his clothes soaked through and his head shaved. Although his friends took him to hospital, he suffered a cardiac arrest and was pronounced brain dead. Other young people to have died after such ceremonies include Gavin Britton at Exeter University, Tom Ward at Hull University and Alex Doji at Staffordshire University.

Universities are aware that these ceremonies take place, know how dangerous they are and most, if not all, forbid those involving excessive drinking. However, some clubs and societies (arguing that it's 'tradition' or a 'harmless rite of passage') respond by carrying them out under the radar. For example, by conducting them off campus or telling students not to tell anyone.

Students, clubs and societies that choose to be involved in banned initiations can face serious consequences:

- In 2018, Northumbria University issued formal warnings and withdrew a number of elite sports scholarships from those involved in the football team's initiation involving alcohol

- Also in 2018, UCL Students' Union shut down its men's rugby club, withdrew its funding, prevented the team from training on the university pitches and removed the team from the university league after team members attempted to hold a banned initiation ceremony

In 2020, BUCS (British Universities Colleges & Sport), the national governing body for higher education sport in the UK, took steps to ensure that students aren't put off playing a sport they love, or trying out a new one, because of a fear of initiations. Students can report a problem initiation – one they've experienced, have heard of or know is upcoming – on an anonymous basis and BUCS will liaise with the university to ensure appropriate action is taken.

With regard to initiations, you have choices:

- You don't have to participate in these types of ceremonies

- You don't have to drink everything or do everything

- If you decide to go then read the advice below on strategies

- If you feel that you'd only be accepted if you joined in, but you really don't want to, then consider looking for an alternative club
  - Look for a similar club or society on campus that doesn't have the same reputation or 'rules'. They might have initiations but ones which are fun rather than cruel, excessive or undignified
  - You could look for the same club or society in the nearest town

Strategies For Managing A Night Out

If you know you're going to be drinking heavily, there are things you can do to manage the impact. These include:

- Having a proper meal and a large glass of water before you start drinking

- Not going crazy at the 'pre' otherwise you'll peak early

- Drinking slowly

- Drinking water or soft drinks throughout the evening as well as alcohol

- Not drinking everything or at every round: refuse it, go to the loo, stay on the dance floor, mix it, replace it with water, spill it or pour it away

- Eating whilst drinking

- Managing yourself: you know how much alcohol you can tolerate so limit yourself to a number of drinks per hour

- Not drinking to the point that you can't make sensible decisions e.g. lose your phone, fall over, vomit, get in a fight, snog someone you'll regret

- Leaving out a large bottle of water by your bed – and drinking it before you go to sleep

Drugs

It's possible that you'll come across drugs at university and you may be invited to take them.

The Risks

There are many risks associated with taking drugs without medical supervision. These include:

- It's illegal therefore the drugs are unregulated: you can never be sure what they contain or what the effects might be
  - To make them go further, they could be mixed with other drugs or toxic substances
  - Or they may be in a purer form and therefore far stronger than something similar that you – or someone you know – have taken previously

- You can't be sure how you might react to them – everyone is different

- There are known links between drug use and mental health problems: either developing a serious mental health disorder or worsening an underlying one

- They can be highly addictive and, over time, a person might have to take the drug just to feel 'normal' and they might have a hard time controlling their need to take the drug
  - Some people might start to feel the need to take more of a drug or take it more often, and it can impact their sleeping and eating patterns and social interactions. They might borrow or steal money to pay for the drugs

- Universities are increasingly carrying out random drug raids in university accommodation – using sniffer dogs, cocaine swabs and body-cams
  - Students found with drugs may be expelled, evicted or arrested

How To Say No

The organisation FRANK provides honest information about drugs. If you're feeling pressured to take drugs – and you don't want to – suggestions from FRANK include:

- Prepare yourself. Think about how you'd like to respond if someone offers you drugs so you know what to say

- Say no firmly but clearly and without making a big deal about it. If someone tries to persuade you, don't feel you have to change your mind (it's also likely the person who's offered you drugs won't be offended if you say no as they may have only offered them out of politeness)

- You're not alone. It's easy to think you're the only one who's not tried drugs but, actually, most young people don't take drugs

- If you're finding it hard to be yourself within your group, take a step back and think about whether it's time to find a new group

Source: www.talktofrank.com
FRANK's confidential helpline, open 24/7, is 0300 123 6600

Smoking/Vaping

Traditional Cigarettes

You know there's nothing good about smoking. Your breath smells, it stains your teeth, it ages your skin, weakens your bones, you smell, it's expensive, it's the largest cause of cancer and it increases your likelihood of a heart attack or stroke.

- Give up smoking. Some people find it difficult to give up, especially as nicotine is addictive. But there's support available to help you: you can access the NHS Quit Smoking service through places such as community pharmacies and NHS GP surgeries

- Put any money you would have spent on cigarettes into a glass pot like a jam jar, and watch it quickly grow. Then reward yourself with something lovely because you deserve it: it's not easy to kick an addiction

Vaping

Vaping allows you to inhale nicotine in a vapour. Although less harmful than smoking conventional cigarettes, they aren't harmless.

- They contain nicotine, which is an addictive substance and one that raises your heart rate

- The vapour contains some potentially harmful chemicals

- There are many unknowns including the long-term impact on health

Don't take up vaping if you're a non-smoker. But if you're trying to stop smoking conventional cigarettes, current government recommendations are that vapes are a useful aid, particularly in conjunction with expert help such as the NHS Quit Smoking Service.

"Everyone is in the same boat as you, so you're definitely not alone in whatever you're feeling."

9

Feeling Stressed, Worried, Overwhelmed, Lonely Or Worse

New Student Blues

Starting university can be an exciting time but even the most confident person can feel some anxiety given the many new situations they'll experience.

It's quite common to feel low at different points in time, for example, when you're missing the good old days – old friends, old routines, having things done for you – or dealing with new challenges such as managing your money, new ways of working, or dealing with flatmate or friendship issues.

Going to university *is* an unusual situation. For eighteen years, most of you will have lived at home with family and friends around you – people who know you inside out. Starting university, however, thrusts you into new surroundings. The workload may be intense, you may have too little (or too much) free time, you're mixing with and trying to find friends amongst people you don't know, you might be having to look after yourself, you might be worrying about money, and you might feel pressure to have a great time.

When I asked, in my research, what first year students liked least about being at university, there were four common themes: study stresses, money worries, feeling overwhelmed, and their emotional wellbeing – particularly feeling lonely, sad and homesick.

Study Stresses

Going to university gives you the opportunity to study, in depth, a subject you're really interested in. When I asked the Freshers in my research what they liked *best* about being at university, this was one of the most frequently mentioned joys of being at university:

"Learning about a subject you love."

"The ability to study the thing you're most passionate about full-time."

"I am genuinely interested in my course. The opportunity to expand and grow your knowledge is amazing."

"Some of the stuff we're learning is incredibly interesting."

"For me personally, free access to the huge range of engineering software and facilities – which would cost a 'civilian' hundreds of thousands."

Most university courses, however, require a considerable amount of work.

- Even when you've taken the subject at A level, a degree is often a step up in terms of content, complexity and volume. First year students in my research said this was one aspect they disliked about being at university:

"The massive workload."

"All the reading!"

"The deadlines – constantly have an exam date in the back of your mind."

- Teaching approaches at university can be different to what you're used to

"The lack of guidance from lecturers."

"The lack of information given about what to include in assignments."

"Very little academic guidance besides reading lists. Lots of responsibility on you."

- Contact time with teaching staff – lectures, seminars, tutorials, labs or practicals – varies widely, usually by course. Having too little free time, or conversely having too much, requires discipline on your behalf

- Class sizes might be large, which can make asking questions difficult

- And the responsibility is now on you to stay organised and focused since teaching staff aren't likely to chase you or monitor your progress

"Be prepared to motivate yourself because teachers won't push you."

"Having to self-motivate to do work as no one chases it up if I don't do it."

Strategies To Help You Manage Your Studies

- Be prepared for teaching to start straight away

"Get your textbooks in advance as the teaching starts very quickly."

"Try to do some of the essential reading before the course starts, this will save you a lot of much needed time."

- Read the background material and do the preparation – the lecture is just one part of the information you need

"Always do the reading before your lecture then you know what the lecturer is talking about."

"Do the prep work, especially for high contact subjects, as you won't have much time to catch up once you start."

- Do attend/watch all your lectures – and definitely follow up what you miss
  - Lectures are normally recorded, enabling you to catch up on any you miss or review content you found confusing
  - Don't get into the habit of missing lectures – it's usually better to be there in person

"Go to your lectures at the start otherwise you will develop a habit of not going."

"Be disciplined since skipping lectures is more addictive than any drug out there."

- Do ask teaching staff and other students for help if you're not sure about something – you're invariably not the only one who didn't understand
  - Small group sessions, such as seminars, are an ideal place to ask questions
  - Sign up for a peer mentor – students in the year above – who can help you with questions about the course

"It is a big adjustment but it's a good one and everyone else is learning the same things as you so, if you're struggling, so are other people."

- And if teaching staff make their slides available after the lecture, you can focus on what's being said, interact and ask questions – as opposed to making copious notes

"Don't spend too much time in lectures taking thorough notes as it's all on Blackboard. Interacting with the lessons is much more productive than writing down everything on the PowerPoint."

- If teaching staff suggests an assignment will take four weeks, that's how much time you're supposed to allocate to it. This gives you time to ask any questions and also gives you wriggle room for inevitable delays e.g. finding and accessing resources, working with other people on team projects, IT challenges

- Don't let assignments stack up – this only adds to the stress

"Do work early so you don't have to be up ridiculous hours to get it done."

"Don't leave all your work to be done just before the deadline, you won't always get away with it like you did at school."

- If appropriate, refer back to your A level resources

- Take advantage of any resources the university offers: from the library and buddy systems to skills workshops e.g. note-making, essay writing, referencing

- Don't plagiarise: universities are known to use sophisticated computer programmes to scan work for evidence of plagiarism

- Keep track of all your deadlines in a planner or diary

- Manage your time carefully if your course is intense
  - Courses such as engineering and medicine often require a lot of hours in class and you'll be left with limited spare time
  - You'll need to be extra organised and focused so there's time to enjoy your life outside your course

- Manage yourself if your course is lesson-light
  - Students on courses with relatively little contact time are expected to undertake a lot of independent study
  - This is a huge change from school or college – where you may have had only a few 'frees' each week – and it might take a little while to get used to being self-directed so that you don't waste time or fall behind on reading or preparatory work
  - In your planner/diary, timetable your reading, research and preparation time rather than have lots of blank spaces that look like free time

"Make a routine. Regularity and routine are very important during your transition from five lessons a day to maybe three or four a week (course depending)."

  - If you feel you can easily manage all your work in the allocated time then perhaps do other things, for example, get a part-time job (good for money and for your CV), learn a language, take up a sport or volunteer to help run a club or society

- Don't spend all your time studying: make time for relaxation and the social aspects of being at university. This is an important part of the university experience and crucial for your mental wellbeing

- Speak to the teaching staff and/or your personal tutor if you feel worried about your course – they're there to support you

"With the academic side, if you struggle, ask for help: your coursemates, lecturers, personal tutor. They're all there to support you and aren't going to turn you away. If they can't help, they'll always point you to people who can."

"Tell your supervisors and tutors as soon as you are struggling so everything doesn't get on top of you."

Online Learning

It's possible your university may combine face-to-face teaching with online learning e.g. delivering large group lectures online and small group sessions, such as seminars, tutorials and practicals, in person.

- Learning online can bring its own challenges
    - You might experience fatigue, a lack of motivation, a feeling of disconnect from your lecturers and coursemates
    - If it's up to you to decide when to watch lectures you could find yourself falling behind
    - You could experience issues that affect your ability to engage online. These could be to do with reading, writing, language or accessibility needs. You could have problems with IT e.g. access to a laptop or phone, the correct software, sufficient data, decent Wi-Fi, how to use the various platforms or software. Maybe you find it difficult to find a quiet place to work

- There are lots of things you can do to enhance your online learning
    - During classes, turn on your camera and unmute your microphone so you feel more connected with your coursemates and your lecturers. Engage fully whenever you can e.g. comment, ask questions
    - Make your working area different from your bed e.g. watch a lecture in the kitchen or in the library
    - If you can choose when to watch your lectures, you need to be disciplined to ensure you watch them
    - Create or join study groups so that you can talk about the course and form friendships with your coursemates
    - Let your lecturer/personal tutor/university support services know if you have any issues that might affect your ability to engage online
    - Take some time to understand how your university's Virtual Learning Environment (VLE) works, how to access course resources remotely and identify virtual support services

And there are some positives to online learning, for example:

- If your lectures are recorded, then you can watch them when it suits you, you can catch up on anything you've missed and you can review content you found confusing

"Online learning has its benefits: access to materials and lecture slides. All our lectures are recorded as standard so you can watch them again, at your convenience."

- If you have any concerns about attending in person, e.g. if you're concerned about your health or the cost, difficulty or time it takes to travel to university, then online learning addresses those aspects

Money Worries

It's not uncommon for students to have money worries.

- This might be the first time that you've had to live on a restricted income and you might find it hard to budget

- Most of you will try to live within your means and attempt to control how much money you borrow

- If you're living away from home, there's likely to be a realisation about how much things cost and how much your parents previously paid for

- And the maintenance loan may not be sufficient – even to pay your rent

In my research, the first year students commonly mentioned the lack of money as one of the main things they disliked about being at university e.g. having to live on a restricted income, the cost of things, building up debts and worrying about how to pay them off. Comments included:

"Living on a budget."

"Being broke 24/7."

"My student loan doesn't even cover my accommodation (£2,000 less than I need for rent alone)."

"How insanely expensive rent is."

"The vision of repaying the loans after graduation."

For some of you, the maintenance loan combined with any other income you have, e.g. parental contribution or savings, may not be sufficient to live on.

- If you have money worries, read Chapter 7: Money – especially the section on scholarships, grants, bursaries and awards, fee waivers and hardship funds.

- There are pots of money available, particularly if you're experiencing financial hardship. You just need to know where to look

Read the section on paying off Government loans. It's important to remember that, the way repayments currently work, many students will repay only a small amount of what they owe and some will repay nothing at all

Feeling Overwhelmed

Since the majority of you will move away from home to attend university, some or all of the domestic tasks must now be done by you.

On top of attending lectures and undertaking coursework, you might now have to be thinking about food choices, doing food shopping, then cooking and washing up; cleaning and laundry; socialising, taking part in sport, training and society events; and keeping up with old friends and possibly a partner from home. Plus, maybe doing paid work too. So it's not unreasonable that you might feel besieged by tasks, overcome with tiredness and feel you have no time to relax.

This sense of being overwhelmed was frequently commented on, in my research, as one of the things that first year students liked least about being at university:

"Stress. Feels like there's not enough time to do everything."

"Never having free time."

"Irregular sleep schedule makes it feel like there are not enough hours in the day to get work done as well as do the things you enjoy."

"Constantly socialising in combination with figuring out your course, travel, cooking and cleaning can be exhausting."

There are various things you can do to help manage your busy schedule better.

- If you're living away from home
    - Learn from your flatmates: what do they cook that's tasty, quick, healthy and easy? What shortcuts do they use?
    - Could you take turns with a flatmate or friend? E.g. preparing and cooking a meal, doing a load of laundry, having a cleaning rota
    - Try online shopping instead of going to the shops. It's much quicker. Although you might need to do it ahead of time as delivery slots might not be available for a few days

- If you know you have a deadline or a test the following day then it's okay to miss one night out – there will be plenty more

- If it seems the coursework is taking you longer than it should, speak to your tutor or investigate workshops or buddy systems. They might be able to suggest tips you could try

- If you're drinking, manage your alcohol intake
    - Don't drink every night and don't drink if you have a deadline or a test the following day – you won't sleep well and it'll affect your performance
    - It's also expensive. Instead, perhaps you could have friends over to watch a film, game or play cards

- If you're doing paid work, could you reduce your hours?
    - If you need the money, read Chapter 7: Money – particularly bursaries, grants, scholarships and awards, fee waivers and hardship funds

- Take occasional rests and time away from everyone and everything
    - It's okay to say no. When your life is very busy, time alone (ideally with the phone off) is good for the soul and can help you re-charge
    - You could listen to music, read for pleasure, watch a bit of TV, maybe do some yoga, go for a run in the fresh air, game or simply potter

"Be kind to yourself. You can't be everywhere doing everything all at once."

"Don't worry about feeling the need to live up to the typical uni student life expectations of constant partying and socialising. It's okay to have a night or two in, or do something less wild."

- This sense of feeling overwhelmed is particularly common amongst

Freshers in the first term when you're acclimatising to university life plus everyone is eager to go out and socialise

- You should find that you get a bit more efficient at domestic tasks
- Hopefully you'll become quicker at doing coursework as you use all the resources that are available
- And the pressure to join in and go to everything should get a bit less as time passes

Loneliness, Sadness And Homesickness

Feeling lonely, sad and homesick are common feelings amongst new students.

Among the first year students in my research, when I asked what they liked least about being at university, there were many responses that focused on their emotional wellbeing. They described feeling sad, lonely and missing home, parents and old friends – particularly in the first few weeks.

Know that you're not alone and, for most students, over time you'll become more settled and those feelings will pass.

There are things that you can do, which could help:

- Talk about how you're feeling: you may find others around you are experiencing the same emotions or they might share how they're dealing with these feelings. Remember: you're all new together

- Join a few clubs or societies. Not only will this provide a distraction but you're likely to make new contacts and friends

    "Throw yourself into stuff that you think you'll enjoy."

- Look on your university website: there may be initiatives specifically aimed at welcoming and integrating new students

- Look after your physical health
  - Eat and drink healthily: this affects us emotionally as well as physically (read Chapter 5: Food & Drink)
  - Get sufficient sleep: not getting enough sleep can affect your ability to concentrate, your ability to memorise things and you're more likely to be irritable and behave impulsively. Try to prepare your mind and body for sleep e.g. have a warm bath or shower, read a book or listen to the radio, turn off screens, write a 'to do' list, do some light stretches, make the room dark and quiet (invest in ear plugs, if necessary)
  - Bathing can be an effort, especially if you're sharing a bathroom, but having a shower (or a bath) can be a good time to clear your head, have some quiet 'me' time and is an important part of taking care of yourself
  - Exercise isn't just good for the body, it can also be a social activity, it helps you sleep, and the endorphins released during exercise can reduce pain and boost happiness. Try to do at least 30 minutes of moderate aerobic activity five days a week – perhaps incorporate it into your daily routine such as walking briskly or cycling to class – and do strength exercises on two or more days a week
  - Cut down on/cut out alcohol, drugs and smoking: read Chapter 8 on why these things are not good for you and why you should cut them down/out – not only for your health but it would help with any financial worries

- Family and old friends
  - Do speak to your family and old friends – they can be a wonderful, reassuring, supportive network. They're likely to be missing you and will be delighted to speak to you
  - Try not to go home too early. Give yourself time to get used to things. Some universities recommend not going home for the first month
  - But, booking a trip home – just knowing that it's planned – can take a bit of pressure off you and lift your spirits

- Instead of going home, you could invite friends and family to visit so you can show them your new surroundings. You might experience a sense of pride showing them your room, the university, the facilities and the local area

- Social media: recognise that it's life through a filter
    - Looking at other people's social media can make you feel low, make you feel bad about yourself and create FOMO (a fear of missing out)
    - When friends' posts show them having the most amazing time at university, you might feel it's only you who's not having #thebesttimeever. As commented on by students in my research:

"It won't be amazing all the time. Don't compare your experience to anyone else because a lot of people only post/talk about the best parts of it."

"Everyone is going through the same thing and not every day will be like what you see on social media and that's okay!!"

    - Remember that people tend to carefully curate their posts e.g. when they're looking their best or they're in a fun place. They don't tend to include the majority of their time: the everyday, the mundane, the boring. They might also be posting positive images as a way of persuading themselves that everything is great – or in the hope of manifesting it
    - Even your own posts might suggest you're having the most brilliant time – even if you're not

- But social media can also be a force for good. For example:
    - It enables you to communicate with other people remotely and helps maintain existing relationships when you're geographically distant from each other – helping you feel less lonely and isolated
    - People commonly discuss, in real life, what they've seen online – so it's something to talk about

- And, because of the anonymity it can offer, you can communicate with other people who have the same interests as you without fear of being stigmatised

- Let the university know if you need support
    - The university lecturers, personal tutors and support staff have seen many of these same struggles before and can help you: they'll listen, make useful suggestions and support you
    - They may be able to offer practical help to immediately relieve any course-related stress e.g. extend a coursework deadline, allow you extra time in exams, offer one-to-one support from a tutor
    - Some universities offer mentoring schemes or support groups
    - There may be student-led support services. Although the students may not be qualified counsellors, you may prefer to talk about problems such as stress and depression with another student
    - Your university might run a Nightline service: an anonymous listening and information service run by students for students
    - Most universities have welfare teams who can provide independent and confidential advice and guidance to students on academic, welfare and personal issues
    - You could approach the staff at the chaplaincy/multi-faith centre

"If you are struggling, please talk to someone. There really are people there to help!"

"Talk to your tutors as soon as things feel uneasy or hard, even if it's not related to your work."

Some good advice from the students in my research about keeping pushing through – especially during what might be a rollercoaster of a first term:

"Remember not everyone is having a great time all the time and it's alright to have some down days, everyone has them."

"Understand that it won't all be smooth sailing. You will have bad days, where all you want is to go home, but you will also have loads and loads of really good days!!"

"I have had ups and downs at university but that forms part of life and it remains an amazing experience."

"Push through it and don't give up too early on into term."

"Don't worry if you don't feel home at first, it will take a while but hang in there for the first term and you will find something that works for you."

"The first term was definitely a rollercoaster, between settling in, socials and the high workload. But it definitely got easier as I got used to what university life would be like for me."

Be kind to yourself. Going to university is a whole new way of being and you're just getting used to it. The first term is likely to be the hardest as you adjust, find your feet and your friends. Don't give up, give it time.

During the Christmas break you'll probably find that you're missing new friends and you're very likely to miss the independence and freedom that you've become used to.

If Things Are More Serious: Getting Professional Help

Whether you have pre-existing mental health needs or you feel that things have escalated to a point where they're affecting your daily life, it's important to know that help is available. Seek help early if you do experience a problem with your mental health at university – you don't need to wait or try to handle things on your own.

"I sought help for my mental health from my uni and, as terrifying as it was to make myself that vulnerable, I'm so glad I did it now and I would recommend any student doing the same."

"As someone who has anxiety, I'd say if you find yourself struggling at university, it's important to reach out. Most universities will have some sort of mental health support but it requires you to recognise that you need help."

"If you've considered therapy, just do it. You've got nothing to lose and better to start earlier than later."

Some possible signs of escalating emotional difficulty could include persistent sadness, anxiety or depression; feelings of apathy towards things you used to enjoy; weight changes; excessive studying or missing lectures and deadlines; increased isolation; poor personal hygiene; hair loss; insomnia or sleeping too much; and self-harm.

There are things you can do, which could help.

- Look on your university website. Most universities have a free and confidential in-house counselling service where you can access professional counsellors, psychotherapists and mental health advisers

- Speak to your GP

- There are external organisations and resources where you can find support and advice, for example:
    - Mind: 0300 123 3393 or email info@mind.org.uk
    - Student Minds: https://www.studentminds.org.uk/findsupport. html or email info@studentminds.org.uk
    - Student Space (led by Student Minds): https://studentspace.org. uk
    - The Samaritans: 116 123 (you can call for FREE anytime from any phone) or email jo@samaritans.org or visit www.samaritans.org

- PAPYRUS HOPELINEUK: 0800 068 4141, text 07860 039967, or email pat@papyrus-uk.org or visit https://papyrus-uk.org
- Students Against Depression: https://www.studentsagainstdepression.org
- NHS web pages e.g. Student Stress; Counselling for Student Mental Health Problems; Every Mind Matters

If you're in crisis now, call 999 or go to your nearest hospital A&E (Accident and Emergency) department

Worried About A Friend

Perhaps a friend has told you they're unhappy or you've noticed some changes in their appearance or behaviour (see possible signs of emotional struggle p131).

- If you're worried about a friend's emotional wellbeing, you could let them know you're concerned about them, ask them how they're feeling and include them in social arrangements – they'll appreciate this

- If they're seriously struggling, however, it's important to know your limits
  - Although you can offer help, you're unlikely to have the expertise, the experience or the resources that a professionally trained person has
  - Also, you shouldn't be your friend's sole source of support and you do need to be clear about how much you can help

- Encourage your friend to speak to their family or other friends, access professional help through the university support team and/or their GP, and/or use the external resources mentioned above

- If you're very concerned for your friend, you could approach a tutor who can make the university support team aware that a student needs help

- Also, it can be stressful supporting someone who has mental health needs so you should make sure that you keep up your own interests and relationships and ensure you're properly supported too
  - You could talk to a friend (who doesn't gossip), your family, get support from the university or use the external resources above

If You're Considering Leaving

If you're very unhappy, feel that you aren't settling at university and are considering leaving, there are things you can do.

- It might help to set a time to review the situation e.g. at the end of term
  - Setting a time may take some pressure off you
  - You might also find that, by then, you're settled; it does take time for everyone to get used to being at university

- If you're able, you should discuss this with your parents so they can support you

- Talk to your personal tutor, department staff or the Student Union welfare team
  - They'll help you explore your options and advise you on your next steps: whether it's ways they can help you right now or whether it's transferring to another course within the same university, changing university or leaving higher education altogether

- If being away from home is the issue then you could consider transferring to a university closer to home

- Perhaps university is right for you but the timing is wrong
  - You may be able to defer for a year, i.e. halt your studies at a point in the year, then return to the same point one year later

- If money is a concern then you could read Chapter 7: Money. You'll find suggestions of how to apply for additional funding but also alternatives to the typical degree. You could also consider studying on a part-time basis

- If you'd like to transfer to a different course or study at a different university it might affect your student loan (if you have one) so you should contact your loan provider

- Check the terms of any government grant you have received since you may have to make repayments if you leave the course early

- And know that university doesn't suit everyone
    - If you decide it's not for you, there are other ways to forge ahead with your career, become successful and be fulfilled
    - Take that same focus and determination that got you into university in the first place and apply it to whatever you decide to do next. Good luck!

10

The Parents' Chapter

Emotional Impact

If your son or daughter moves away from home to attend university, it can be difficult for you, emotionally.

You may have witnessed them becoming more independent as they reached 18. They may have started (legally) going to bars and nightclubs; they may have passed their driving test and started driving themselves and their friends to places (scary); they may have started earning their own money and making their own purchases (great – although some you might disapprove of); and they may have headed off to festivals and holidays with their friends (more worry).

But parents are on the periphery of these full and busy lives and you may have been used to – and enjoyed – the noise and excitement that comes with older teenagers.

Also, the focus has been sharply on them throughout A levels and then Results Day.

If the offer of a university place was conditional on achieving certain grades then, after getting their results, there's a flurry of activity, which includes:

- Confirming their place at university
    - If they got the results they needed then accepting an offer from their first (firm) or back-up (insurance) choice university
    - If they didn't get the results they needed, they may have chosen an alternative course or university through UCAS Clearing

- Followed by the emails from the university

- The emails concerning finances

- If they're leaving home, there's the excitement (and fear) surrounding where they'll be living and who their new flatmates will be

- Followed by all the preparing and shopping, which you (and your credit card) are likely to be heavily involved in. Hundreds of pounds and many hours are likely to be spent on getting all their stuff together (see the lists of suggested items throughout this guide)

- And then they're saying goodbye to friends and family
    - If their friends are going to a variety of universities, the start dates will vary therefore farewell parties will extend over several weeks
    - And, if they're moving away from a partner, then they're likely to want to spend a lot of time with him or her before they leave

With Results Day being just a month or so before they leave, a lot happens in a very short space of time.

And then they're gone.

Staying Connected

If your son or daughter leaves home, how much contact you have with them will vary according to their personality and their experience of being at university.

- If they're naturally a bit more cautious, or if they're finding things a bit hard, then they might contact you frequently – particularly in the beginning – looking for reassurance whilst they get used to university life

- Be positive for them. If they feel lonely, sad or homesick, reassure them that they're not the only one feeling this way, their new life will settle down and things will get better. You could suggest they read Chapter 9

- Maybe they want less contact because they're relishing the independence and freedom that comes from living away from home. They're enjoying finding things out for themselves

- Or maybe they're simply too busy to call or text, especially at the beginning
    - In the first few weeks they're spending time getting to know their new flatmates; going to various events, especially during Freshers' Week; probably going to bed late and then getting up late; making some or all of their own meals – which requires planning, shopping, cooking and cleaning up
    - If they've joined clubs and societies then they're attending the events associated with these interests and going to training sessions if they're sporty
    - They're keeping up with old friends
    - And, if they're in an existing relationship, it will require significant time and commitment to keep it going from a distance
    - Oh, and they've started their course and are working on assignments
    - Life is full on. And you might be low on the 'need to contact' list

- It's possible that the occasional contact you receive might be purely functional in nature e.g. they need to know how to do something or ask if you would pay for something and, as soon as you've explained/resolved it, they may need to go

- You should call and text them occasionally so they know that you're thinking of them
    - You can use social media, e.g. set up a family WhatsApp or Twitter, for everyone to communicate through, and ask them to post the occasional text or photo so you know they're alive
    - You could ask to be accepted as a Friend or Follower on social media so you can see their posts (they may refuse)

- You could set a regular date and time to speak

But the ball is really in their court.

As the weeks pass, their lives calm down and become a bit more routine, you might find that you get more regular contact. Which is nice.

Help For Sad Parents

When a child leaves home for university, parents might experience a sense of loss, similar to grief.

You're used to having them around, you're used to their noise and mess and you're used to being asked for, or about, things. Now contact may be irregular, missing completely, or you may be worried about how they're coping.

As long as you get the sense they're settling in, then the focus should now be on you. You could:

- Talk to other parents whose children have also left for university: share your experiences, they're likely to be similar and they might have some useful coping strategies

- Join support groups – either in real life or online – for parents of new students (see End Notes for a useful Facebook group)

- Try not to be sad when you speak to your child
    - Be positive and reassuring if they're feeling a bit wobbly
    - Try not to transfer your own sadness or anxiety

- Start enjoying the freedom that one less child brings e.g. focus on your career, spend more time with your partner, see friends more often, start a new project, fill your life with enjoyable things

- After the initial shock, you do get used to them not being around – the new normal

- And you will still see them
    - They may come back occasionally during term time for family or friends' events or simply to rest and recharge
    - And the holidays are frequent and long

Help For Worried Parents

For most parents, there's nothing worse than seeing your child distressed or unhappy.

- If they tell you they're feeling sad, lonely, homesick or overwhelmed, these are common emotions amongst new students (read Chapter 9 to see they're not alone – and suggestions for what to do). Things do tend to settle down and they do normally get better

- If they're feeling isolated, encourage them to make or join study groups and club/society/interest groups. This will enable them to interact with people with similar interests to them and attend fun or interesting events

- If you're concerned your son or daughter is struggling and needs extra support, encourage them to speak to their personal tutor or student support services
  - They're familiar with these types of worries and can give good advice and strategies for dealing with their concerns

- If they've moved away from home, encourage them to stay at the university rather than come home often – some universities recommend students don't go home during the first month

- If they continue to struggle, maintain regular contact and perhaps set a deadline, for example, at the end of term, to review the situation

- If your son or daughter has told you something or is behaving in a way that's particularly worrying then you should contact the university
  - Student mental health is taken seriously and there's usually an email address or a telephone number on the university's website for worried parents
  - The university will normally arrange for someone from the student welfare department to contact your son or daughter
  - Call 999 if you feel it's life-threatening

Financial Implications

If your son or daughter is eligible, and they require it, they can apply to the UK government for a tuition fee loan plus a maintenance loan to go towards living costs.

- How much maintenance loan they get depends on various factors e.g. where they're studying, whether they're living at home or not, whether they're studying full- or part-time

- The maintenance loan is partly based on the family household income so there's an implicit expectation that families should contribute towards their child's living costs

- As a guide, you could make up the shortfall between the maintenance loan that your son or daughter receives and the maximum maintenance loan
    - For example, if the maximum maintenance loan for a full-time undergraduate student from England, living away from home and outside London is £9,500 but your child only receives £6,500 in maintenance loan then you could, if you're able, contribute £3,000 per year towards their living costs

- If you're able to contribute more, this would be helpful since many students find it difficult to live on this level of income

Having a son or daughter at university might be financially difficult for you. You may not be in a position to contribute towards their living costs but you do need to have this conversation with your son or daughter in advance: how much, if anything, you can give them and how often they will receive it

- Since the maintenance loan they receive may not be sufficient to even pay their rent, you should discuss other ways they could support themselves (see Chapter 7: Money). There are pots of money out there and this chapter shows your son or daughter where to look for them

- In general, it's not recommended that you take out a personal loan to help your child with their student debt. This is almost always a more expensive option than your child taking out a student loan – since interest rates on student loans are still relatively low and, crucially, they only need to repay the loan if they earn enough

Follow this link for a handy student finance calculator for students from England or the EU starting a new undergraduate course. It estimates student loans and extra state funding. The result will be more accurate if you know your annual household income:

- www.gov.uk/student-finance-calculator

Follow these links for information on UK government student loans:

- England: www.gov.uk/student-finance
- Scotland: www.saas.gov.uk
- Wales: www.studentfinancewales.co.uk
- Northern Ireland: www.studentfinanceni.co.uk
- Jersey: https://www.gov.je/working/careers/16to19yearolds/ enteringhighereducation/financinghighereducationcourses/Pages/index. aspx
- Guernsey: https://www.gov.gg/studentfinance
- Isle of Man: https://www.gov.im/student-grants

Weekend And Holiday Visits: What To Expect

You're looking forward to seeing them, having them home and hearing all about university life…

- They might turn up tired, grumpy or emotional

- A calm home might become chaotic: there might be squabbling with siblings, arguments over use of the car, loud music playing, doors banging, queues for the bathroom and no food in the fridge

- You might see very little of them. If they're exhausted (physically and emotionally) they might simply want to sleep, they might have come home to see old friends or a partner, they might want to just spend time with the dog

- They might behave as if they're still at university: coming and going at all hours or just staying in their room

> *They might not want to conform to old rules. They've tasted freedom and they've learnt to live independently of you*

- You'll probably have to negotiate new ways of living together:
    - Have a conversation about what you'd like them to do, how you'd like them to behave or what things you'd like help with whilst they're at home
    - Consider not setting curfews but ask them to let you know if they're coming home late, having friends to stay or not coming home at all
    - You can set mutually respectful house rules, e.g. being quiet when others are sleeping
    - Remind them that you and their siblings would like to see them too – so to set some afternoons or evenings aside to catch up

> *You should let them set their own schedules - as they're used to doing at university. If you're too stifling, you run the risk of them returning to university early or not wanting to come home at all*

- They're probably missing home comforts
    - They're very likely to enjoy some favourite meals, with any leftover portions sent back to university with them

- If they're trying to save money, they might bring home large bags of laundry

- You might see them noticeably relaxing into their own bed
  - If you can, it's helpful if their bed or bedroom remains theirs so that they have somewhere secure and comforting to come home to during this time of intense change

- Hopefully you get the sense they're settling in to their new life
  - You might notice, over the Christmas break, that they talk a lot about their new friends and their new life and, by January, they might be keen to reclaim their independence
  - After a few days or weeks of having them home, you too might be looking forward to them reclaiming their independence ;)

- Christmas and Easter holidays are long: usually lasting around four weeks
  - It's possible that your son or daughter might feel a little anxious about going back to university after such a long break: reconnecting with friends who are still quite new to them, returning to exams, anticipating the chores they'll need to do if they live away from home
  - Be positive for them: talk about all the good things they've mentioned about being at university. It's likely that, after just a few days of being back at university, they'll be completely at ease again
  - If they're returning by car, and if you're able, they'll probably appreciate some food supplies to see them through the first few days

NB Half terms tend not to be the norm at university. Some have Reading Weeks mid-way through the term but the university may expect students to stay, in order to do preparatory work or catch up on reading.

Useful Things To Do Before They Leave

If your son or daughter is leaving home, you can take practical steps to help them prepare for independent living. For example:

- Teach them some basic cookery skills, especially meals that are healthy, tasty, quick and easy

- Show them how to do laundry – at least how to use the washing machine

- Share some cleaning tips

- Talk to them about how to choose accommodation e.g. weekly cost, distance from university

- Talk to them about finances e.g. apportioning money, looking for bargains in supermarkets, utility bills, student travel cards, overdrafts, the difference between debit and credit cards, and how to find more money (read Chapter 7: Money)

- Talk to them about how they might feel during the first term e.g. euphoric, sad, happy or overwhelmed – and they might experience all of those emotions at different times. Explain that the first term is likely to be hardest in terms of settling in but to keep going, if they can, and to seek help if they need it (read Chapter 9)

- Encourage them to read this book before they leave :)

End Notes

Countdown to Leaving

UCAS dates https://www.ucas.com/

Introduction

HESA. First year higher education (HE) student enrolments by level of study

https://www.hesa.ac.uk/data-and-analysis/sb258/figure-1

Chapter 2 – Important Things To Do Before The Start Of Term

Gov.uk. Student Finance

https://www.gov.uk/apply-for-student-finance

The Tab. How much will Freshers week cost at your uni?

https://thetab.com/2015/09/14/revealed-the-cost-of-freshers-week-53498

Gov.uk. TV Licence

https://www.gov.uk/tv-licence

NHS. Getting Medical Care as a Student

https://www.nhs.uk/nhs-services/getting-medical-care-as-a-student/

Chapter 3 – Your Living Arrangements

University friends: By chance or by design? By Martin Rosenbaum Freedom
of information specialist @rosenbaum6 8th December 2018

https://www.bbc.co.uk/news/education-46430204

Chapter 5 – Food & Drink

NHS. The Eatwell Guide

https://www.nhs.uk/live-well/eat-well/the-eatwell-guide/

Chapter 6 – Friendships & Relationships

Tea Consent https://www.youtube.com/watch?v=fGoWLWS4-kU

Copyright ©2015 Emmeline May and Blue Seat Studios

NHS. Contraception Guide. Emergency contraception (morning after pill,
IUD), 2018

https://www.nhs.uk/conditions/contraception/emergency-contraception/

Chapter 7 – Money

Save the Student. Student living costs in the UK

https://www.savethestudent.org/money/student-budgeting/what-do-
students-spend-their-money-on.html

GOV.UK. Student Finance – new full time students

https://www.gov.uk/student-finance/new-fulltime-students

NHS BSA. Low Income Scheme

https://www.nhsbsa.nhs.uk/nhs-low-income-scheme

NHS. Save Money With a Prescription Prepayment Certificate (PPC)

https://www.nhs.uk/nhs-services/prescriptions-and-pharmacies/save-money-with-a-prescription-prepayment-certificate-ppc/

The Scholarship Hub

https://www.thescholarshiphub.org.uk/over-150-million-worth-of-scholarships-uk-students/

GOV.UK. Higher and Degree Apprenticeships https://www.gov.uk/government/publications/higher-and-degree-apprenticeships

Chapter 8 – Staying Safe At University

Ian Johnson, Chronicle Live, 28th December 2018

Tony Diver and Georgia Gee, The Telegraph, 7th December 2018

BUCS. Reporting an Initiation

https://www.bucs.org.uk/report-an-initiation.html

Vaping in England: 2021 evidence update summary

https://www.gov.uk/government/publications/vaping-in-england-evidence-update-february-2021/vaping-in-england-2021-evidence-update-summary

Chapter 10 – The Parents' Chapter

On Facebook: Parents of Current & Prospective University Students in the UK

https://facebook.com/groups/445099209314208

About The Author

Melissa Scallan is a writer, adviser and speaker specialising in higher education.

She's an adviser to UCAS, speaks about the student experience at higher education conferences and gives reassuring and informative talks to sixth form students about preparing for university.

As a journalist and a researcher, with a Master's degree in psychology from the LSE, Melissa's work is carefully researched and thoughtfully presented to prioritise the wellbeing of students as they embark on this life-changing step into higher education.

Acknowledgements

Particular thanks must go, once again, to Louise Salmon for her kindness, careful and thoughtful editing and continuing enthusiasm and to Molly Shields for her positivity, her wonderful illustrations and for making this book look so fantastic. And to Mark, Katie and Ellie who've put up with me being focused on this book. For years!

Many, many people have helped me with this book. Family and good friends have given me encouragement, sent me relevant information, shared experiences, given me advice, forwarded the research questionnaire and proofread. And the organisations that I approached for advice and information have been so helpful and supportive too. Thank you.

A Request From The Author

Thank you for buying Starting University – I hope you've found it helpful. Please would you consider writing a review, wherever you purchased it from? – reviews are valuable and I'd be very grateful. Thank you.

Printed in Great Britain
by Amazon